Hold That Thought

52

Thoughtful Reflections For Your Year

Words by **Ronan Scully**

Photographs by **Andrew Downes**

Edited by Hilary Martyn, PJ Cunningham and Adam Brophy

Design and Layout Niamh Carey, Liz White Designs

ISBN 978-0-9563541-4-3

© Ronan Scully, 2010

BWP Ltd., 1-5 North Frederick Street, Dublin 1

Printed in the Republic of Ireland.

Photo list

Title Page – Dewy Morning; p3 – Teardrops; p6 – Unchained; p12 – Roll On; p16 – From Clare To Here; p26 – The Last Marble; p30 – A Lovely Smile; p34 – Puppy Love; p39 – The Windy Burren; p46 - Icicles; p49 – Route 66; p56 – Pebbles; p61 – Stairway; p64 – Dewy Morning; p66 – Debs Girl; p70 – Sarah's Feet; p74 – Crinniu; p78 – Brothers And Sisters; p84 – The Praying Hands; p87 – Solitude; p102 – Ollie; p107 - Jaime; p109 – The Beautiful Doll; p116 – At The Crossroads; p121 - Zell Am See; p126 – Natures Gift; p130 – The Three Trees; p136 – Sunnyside Out; p142 – Dream Waves; p147 – Pear Drop; p150 – A Helping Hand

---

Contents

FOREWORD
An Taoiseach, Brian Cowen T.D.

For both the author Ronan and the photographer Andrew, helping people in need is an integral part of their family life. Their parents emphasised from an early age how important this was and over the years instilled in them a sense of passion for helping people less well off than themselves, as well as a recognition for and solid defence of people's human rights.

From an early age and on a personal level I knew that Ronan's outlook on life would be one of helping and caring for people. I recall when speaking at an event in Clara, when I was only a wet week in the Dáil as a young TD, being hugely impressed and in some awe with Ronan heading off to help Mother Teresa's Missionaries of Charities in Bucharest, Romania and GOAL in Calcutta, India.

Ronan and Andrew are absolutely committed to their chosen careers and charities and their integrity and compassion comes across strongly in this wonderful and well-crafted book. I wish them both every success with this project and their chosen charities. I have no doubt this is but the start of an exciting collaborative process and that we will be hearing much more from them over the years.

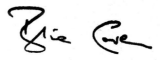

MESSAGE FROM THE AUTHOR
Ronan Scully

Ronan Scully is a humanitarian worker with the charity GOAL and is based in the west of Ireland. He has been writing 'Thoughts for the week', for a few years and has been lucky enough to have his own column for a period of time in *The Irish Catholic* and *The Galway Independent* newspapers for which he is most grateful.

I was delighted when my good friend Andrew Downes agreed to support me on this project to raise funds for charity by taking some fantastic, thoughtful photographs to compliment most of the written thoughts on the following pages. I was also equally delighted when Hilary Martyn of *The Galway Independent* and PJ Cunningham of *The Sunday Tribune* agreed to edit the thoughts and layout of the book for me. I would also like to thank my friends, Taoiseach Brian Cowen and journalist and broadcaster Ralph O'Gorman for their foreword and introduction. I would like to dedicate this book to my wife Jacqui and my daughter Mia and to all my family, friends and colleagues who have supported me in some way throughout my life.

I would also like to dedicate this book to the memory of my close and dear friend Donal Rabbette who I will hold forever in my thoughts.

Ronan Scully

MESSAGE FROM THE PHOTOGRAPHER
Andrew Downes

Andrew Downes is a freelance press photographer based in the west of Ireland.

I was delighted when Ronan Scully asked me to contribute to this book and enjoyed the challenge of creating evocative images to compliment the thought-provoking words of my friend. I am particularly delighted that a portion of the funds raised by this publication will support the work of the Irish Guide Dogs for the Blind, which my father, Frank Downes, has supported for over 30 years. I would like to thank my family, friends and of course Ollie for their modelling skills!

Andrew Downes

See www.andrewdownes.net for further details on Andrew's photography work.

THE EDITORS

PJ Cunningham

PJ Cunningham is the Deputy Editor and Sports Editor of *The Sunday Tribune* and has been involved in helping GOAL and other charities over the years. PJ is a former Clara clubmate and colleague of the author, Ronan Scully. Having helped Ronan become the top scorer for the team by unselfishly laying off every pass to him (not strictly true), PJ is now happy to help put in the odd semi-colon to ensure Ronan scores another goal with this great book.

Hilary Martyn

Hilary Martyn is the editor of *The Galway Independent* newspaper. She was delighted to be asked to assist in editing this book as, through her position with *The Galway Independent*, she has been very active in supporting GOAL's and some other charities' fundraising efforts over the years, assisting in a fundraising drive for tsunami swept Indonesia in 2004 and earthquake devastated Haiti earlier this year. *The Galway Independent* is a free weekly newspaper with a circulation of over 58,000 copies which are distributed throughout Galway city and county every Wednesday. It is also available online at www.galwayindependent.com.

INTRODUCTION

It is our good fortune, yet not surprising, that Ronan Scully should gather his noble thoughts and Andrew Downes his evocative photographs and present them in book form. After all, much of Ronan's work has already been published in *The Irish Catholic* and *The Galway Independent* newspapers. For Ronan Scully's thoughts are invariably optimistic and enriching, always thoughtful and positive yet provocative. They make one feel good about oneself, about life, confident even, in the increasingly unsafe environment in which we live.

The charities chosen to benefit from the sale of this publication, GOAL, Irish Guide Dogs for the Blind, Alan Kerins Projects, and Dóchas Cancer Care, tell their own story. All are humanitarian causes, humanitarian just like the author himself.

The artistry of Andrew Downes' photographs adds immeasurably to the production, captures perfectly the essence of the various thoughts and sits comfortably beside each story as if to say 'hold that thought'.

The contents are a pure treasure trove of wonderful titles, some straightforward and others that whet the imagination. The straightforward or obvious ones might include 'Wishing For Peace In The World', 'A Little Bit Of Kindness Can Go A Long Way', 'A Christmas Story' and many others. There are a total of 52 short stories contained herein.

But what captures my imagination are the more obscure and inventive titles such as 'Time And The Thousand Marbles', 'The Littlest Policeman's Last Wish', 'The Empty Egg' and 'Keep Your Fork, The Best Is Yet To Come'. I look forward to challenging myself to second guess the author's punch line. Best not to hold one's breath!

This book is essentially inspired by the integrity of Ronan Scully but the breadth and depth of the content is probably based on the capacity for fun and mischief of the same Ronan Scully! It is what makes the book a good and balanced read.

The book is an excellent work of penmanship, relevant and meaningful but always enjoyable. The photographs are thoughtful and evocative.

Hold that thought, try to hold all the thoughts, it's worth the effort.

Ralph O'Gorman

Broadcaster and journalist
Galway

MESSAGE FROM THE FOUR CHARITIES

GOAL, Irish Guide Dogs for the Blind, Alan Kerins Projects and
Dóchas Cancer Care

GOAL

www.goal.ie

GOAL is indebted to the Irish public whose constant generosity
and compassion has made it possible for us to respond to nearly
every major natural and man-made disaster and operate
development programmes in over 50 countries since our
inception. GOAL works towards ensuring that the poorest
and most vulnerable in our world and those affected by
humanitarian crises have access to the fundamental needs and
rights of life such as food, water, shelter, medical attention and
primary education.

Today GOAL spends millions every year implementing relief, rehabilitation and
development programmes to help the most vulnerable in 11 developing countries.
GOAL is proud of the fact that we have kept our administration costs exceptionally
low for almost 33 years. Thank you for your help in supporting GOAL.

Irish Guide Dogs for the Blind

www.guidedogs.ie

Irish Guide Dogs for the Blind, established in 1976, helps
people who are blind, visually impaired and disabled
achieve independence and dignity through our world class
guide dog and ancillary services. 90 per cent of our funding
comes from voluntary fundraising and contributions
through the hard work and dedication of over 100 volunteer branches with thousands
of fundraising volunteers enabling us to deliver these services.

As well as our guide dog service to people who are blind and visually impaired, we
also offer orientations and mobility (long cane) training and independent living skills.
We also support a child mobility programme. In addition, we offer assistance dogs to
families of children with autism. All our services have offered clients a mobility and
independence to enhance their lives. Thank you for your help in supporting the Irish
Guide Dogs for the Blind.

Alan Kerins Projects

www.alankerins.ie

We at the Alan Kerins Projects are proud to work with the most disadvantaged and poorest of the poor in Zambia, Africa, by offering hope, commitment, dedication and unique friendships to better their lives. The enthusiasm and ongoing support we receive fuels our passion by allowing us offer a light of hope to the vulnerable and orphaned in Africa. Without your help these children would be forgotten. We work with the people on the ground ensuring that thousands of families benefit in every possible way. We put our hearts and energy into building up communities through housing, schools, medicine and sport.

We are proud of what we do and the most important result we have achieved is giving the vulnerable the opportunity to actively participate in their lives with dignity. Thank you for your help with the Alan Kerins Projects.

Dóchas Cancer Care

www.dochasoffaly.ie

DÓCHAS
Offaly Cancer Support Group

Dóchas is a place designed to support you and your loved ones as you deal with the presence of cancer in your life. For over ten years we've helped many like you throughout the Midlands and beyond. Our aim is to care for you in a holistic manner with treatments that nurture your physical, mental, spiritual and emotional wellbeing. Whether it is massage or music, a chat or counselling, find out what suits you.

We want to help you and your family come to terms with your illness at your own pace. Dóchas believes you can regain some of the control back in your life during this extremely difficult and draining time. Our service is 100 per cent confidential and your care remains our focus. Our services complement primary medical care. You'll get to meet many people just like you who also go about their daily lives while undertaking this huge challenge.

So, whether you've been recently diagnosed or cancer is affecting your family's life on a daily basis, call in to us for a chat and a cuppa. Genuine support is closer than you think. Drop in to see us at www.dochasoffaly.ie.

ACKNOWLEDGEMENTS

I would like to thank my close friend Andrew Downes for agreeing to publish this book in partnership with me and for taking some wonderful and insightful photographs to enhance my thoughts.

For all their advice and comments and for never allowing me to lose my focus on the various thoughts I was writing and the reflective photographs that Andrew was taking, we would like to thank our editors Hilary Martyn, PJ Cunningham and Adam Brophy. We would also like to thank our wonderful wives Jacqui and Anna and our children Mia, Sophie, Roan, Alice and Lily for instilling the courage in us to put these thoughts and photographs on paper and for believing in us from the beginning. Also, Garry O'Sullivan, editor of The Irish Catholic newspaper, who was the first to take a chance on my 'Thoughts' and put some of them to print for his newspaper. I am greatly indebted to him.

I would like to thank John O' Connor and his team of Paula and Adam from Blackwater Press for believing in us and for supporting us in making this dream come through. I would also like to thank Taoiseach Brian Cowen and broadcaster/ journalist Ralph O'Gorman for their kind foreword and introduction. We would also like to thank Paul Galvin, Fr Niall Ahern, Ricey Scully and Frank Downes for their valued opinions. And to Fr Colm Hogan, Fr Eamon Kelly, Fr Adrian McGrath, Fearghal Murphy, Ritchie Donovan, Fr Colm Riedy and Fr David Cribben for their help and support.

Finally, I would like to thank all our families, friends and colleagues who were and are a great source of inspiration to us in everything we do in life and we hope and pray that we will someday be able to repay them for all their love and support.

Ronan Scully

1.

Be The Change

*M*ahatma Gandhi believed that we must be the change we want to see in the world. This was well demonstrated when he helped India gain its independence. Gandhi was a revolutionary man, but he accomplished India's emergence as a nation without starting a revolution. In fact, he advocated no violence. One of the most powerful countries in the world yielded to the commitment of one man and the dream of millions.

What change can we affect?

In order for things to change, you have to change. We can't change others; we can only change ourselves. However, when we change, it changes everything. And in doing so, we truly can be the change we want to see in the world.

We live in peculiar times. More communication devices than ever before connect us, yet more people live alone. We want to belong to communities, but our cities can be very lonely places. We buy more and more things with more and more money, but they don't make us happy. Life satisfaction was higher during post-war rationing in the 1940s. The rich are getting richer, but nearly ten per cent of Irish people are shockingly poor. The other 90 per cent experience other kinds of poverty. Most of us feel that our lives are missing something. Membership in political parties and unions continues to decline, yet tens of thousands of Irish people took to the streets to protest the war on Iraq and Irish people raised millions of euros for tsunami relief.

We feel things very deeply and we want to do something, but sometimes the scale of the issues makes it difficult for us. We ask ourselves: 'How can I make a difference? What can I do? How can I be the change?' And we resign ourselves to the preconceived notion that nothing we do will make a difference anyway and on we go.

First steps

Changing the self is how one can 'be the change'. Always remember that this is your world, the things that happen here are directly affected by you. There are no ordinary moments, there are no trivial actions. Everything you do, everything you say (or don't say) matters. Look at every action and reaction and ask yourself: 'Am I being the change I want to see in the world?'

Part of the human condition seems to be a desire to accomplish noble acts, to be the change, to inspire others to greatness. A fireman rushes into a burning building to rescue a mother and child. A soldier jumps between his comrade and a dangerous land mine. A child climbs a tree to rescue a pet cat. In every walk of life people seek to find ways to be needed, to be important to others, to accomplish things that will benefit mankind.

Our outer world is a mirror of our inner world, with no exceptions. To change our outer world, we must start with our inner world. If you want more prosperity, be more generous and be open to receive generosity from others. If you want more love, be more loving and be more open to receiving love. Stop judging others and practise acceptance and compassion. We cannot change others, only ourselves. Instead of pushing against what others are doing that you perceive to be wrong, focus on yourself.

Gandhi wasn't alone

The following is inscribed on the tomb of an Anglican Bishop in Westminster Abbey (1100 AD): 'When I was young and free and my imagination had no limits, I dreamed of changing the world. As I grew older and wiser, I discovered the world would not change, so I shortened my sights somewhat and decided to change only my country. But it too seemed immovable. As I grew into my twilight years, in one last desperate attempt, I settled for changing only my family, those closest to me, but alas they would have none of it. And now, as I lie on my deathbed, I suddenly realise, if I had only changed myself first, then by example I would have changed my family. From their inspiration and encouragement, I would then have been able to better my country and, who knows, I may have even changed the world.'

Thought for the week

As your thought for week one, be the change for good you wish to see in your world.

Acceptance

*'God grant me the serenity to accept the things I cannot change, courage
to change the things I can, and wisdom to know the difference.'*

Acceptance is the key to the Serenity Prayer, commonly recited at Twelve Steps addiction group meetings. If we can understand what this prayer means, then we can better understand what recovery from addiction and worry is about.

As humans, we have two basic strategies for handling any situation that disturbs us. One is to change the situation. For example, if we are short of a few bob, we can trim our latte or cream bun allowance or seek an increase in our weekly pay. If we are lonely, we can call a loved one. This is how we usually cope with our anguish and distress. We try to alter the world outside us. And in many cases, this is powerful and appropriate.

However, circumstances are sometimes beyond our power. A sudden, unpredicted expense might undercut our plans to save money. We can call a friend or a loved one to suppress our loneliness, but that person may not be at home. Hoping we can control every event that comes our way is like hoping we can control the weather or how many goals Wayne Rooney will score for England.

Options

In such moments, we often forget we have a second option. We can change our response to the situation. Viktor Frankl was prisoner number 119104 in a concentration camp in the Second World War. He spent most of his time alone, laying tracks for railway lines. Most people assume he would have been miserable or gone insane, but, even in the concentration camp, Frankl felt free. In his book *Man's Search for Meaning*, he concluded that everything can be taken from us except our ability to choose our attitude in any given set of circumstances. Another name for this freedom is acceptance. And acceptance is the key to the Serenity Prayer.

Frankl discovered this second option while he was in the concentration camp. Escape was not feasible; he was powerless over his situation. So he responded by dwelling on thoughts that empowered him. More specifically, Frankl stayed alive to the beauty of nature. Even the Nazis could not take away sunsets. He imagined amusing incidents that could take place in the future, allowing him to laugh. And he remembered the people he loved. He wrote how a man who has nothing left in this world may still know bliss, if only for a brief moment, in the contemplation of the people and things he loved and in the good he did in his life.

Applying serenity to our lives

Complete this sentence: 'I would be happy if I had ...' Typical answers include the right job, the right relationship, a new car, a child, a house. All of these have to do with the first option: having the right circumstances. All are attempts to change the world outside our heads.

For example, addiction is something we are powerless over and recovery from addiction means looking for serenity elsewhere – in the world inside our heads. Recovery hinges on learning to dwell on beliefs, attitudes and thoughts that remain true no matter what happens to us. The most important thing to learn and to remember is that there is always another way of looking at anything.

Remember

The Serenity Prayer reminds us that we should change what we can, accept that which we cannot change and strive to know the difference. For people in recovery, for all of us, such knowledge is the heart of serenity. The Serenity Prayer offers us more than an insightful look back at our past; it provides us with a road map for our future.

Thought for the week

As your thought for the week, pray for people you know who have an addiction or a worry in their lives, that they will say the Serenity Prayer and use it as a road map for their future and that they will or we will have the courage and wisdom to use that map in our future dealings with ourselves and with others.

3

If You Are At War, You Can't Be At Peace

To forgive means to give up, to let go. When we forgive, we give up revenge and let go of resentment. We restore our faith, not only in ourselves, but in life itself. If you are at war with others, you cannot be at peace with yourself.

Let it go

We have all been hurt and wounded by the actions or words of others. Sometimes, the grievances have been so great we thought, 'No way, this I cannot forgive!' Resentment and hostility can run so deep that forgiveness becomes very difficult. We feel we have a right to our indignation. However, living with resentment takes so much effort. It creates a tremendous void in and around us. All the poisonous feelings of hatred and resentment stay bottled up inside and eventually they ooze into all the areas of our life. We become bitter, angry, unhappy and frustrated.

Forgiveness helps us move forward. It benefits the one who forgives more than the one who is forgiven. It is often the key to our happiness. However, forgiving someone takes moral courage. It means choosing to let go and move on, and favouring the positive over the negative. Forgiveness breaks the cycle of hatred, resentment, anger and pain that is often passed on to those around us. Forgiveness helps us make peace with our past and create a new future!

The two brothers

Two brothers who lived on adjoining farms fell into conflict. It was the first serious rift in years of farming side by side, sharing machinery, and trading labour and goods as needed. The rift began with a small misunderstanding but grew into a major difference. One morning there was a knock on the older brother's door. He opened it to find a man with a carpenter's toolbox.

'I'm looking for a few days work,' the man said. 'Perhaps you would have a few small jobs here and there. Could I help you?'

'Yes,' said the older brother. 'I do have a job for you. Look across the creek at that farm. That's my younger brother's farm. Last week there was a meadow between us and he took his bulldozer to the river levee and now there is a pond between us. He did this to spite me, but I'll go one better.

'See that pile of lumber curing by the barn? I want you to build me a ten-foot fence, so I won't need to see his place anymore.'

The carpenter said, 'I think I understand the situation. Show me the nails and the post-hole digger and I'll be able to do a job that pleases you.'

The older brother had to go to town for supplies, so he helped the carpenter get the materials ready and was off.

When the farmer returned around sunset, he couldn't believe his eyes. There was no fence there at all; the carpenter had built a bridge stretching from one side of the pond to the other! And when he looked again, he saw that his brother was coming across the bridge, his hand outstretched.

'You are quite a fellow to build this bridge after all I've said and done,' he said. The two brothers met at the middle of the bridge, taking each other's hands. They turned to see the carpenter hoist his toolbox on his shoulder.

'No, wait! Stay a few days. I've a lot of other projects for you,' said the older brother.

'I'd love to stay on,' the carpenter said, 'but I have so many more bridges to build.'

Thought for the week

As your thought for this week, look at the situations in your life where bridges need to be built and try to build them as best you can.

4

Don't Leave It Too Late

It is hard to accept the death of a loved one, especially when you didn't have a chance to say goodbye and it seems like an irreplaceable part of your world is gone. Sometimes you never truly understand grief until it hits you hard in the face. The grief and the pain can be unbearable. You never really know what it's like until you are there yourself, but you look to God because he's the only one who can comfort you.

A sudden loss, such as the death of my friend Donal a few years ago, makes one realise the brevity of life. We often take life for granted. His death made me sit down and reflect. It made me take time to appreciate the loved ones in my life because I don't know what tomorrow will bring. It made me put things in perspective. I want to live life and love it; I don't want to spend my life being unhappy or dissatisfied. I want to put a smile on my face and indeed on others' faces because that's what can make a dark day seem bright.

For those who can identify with me in grief, make it your aim to try to look past it and move on. My friend is gone; I cannot bring him back but, at least in memory of him, I can live a life that I know he would be proud of.

Death opens our eyes, showing us that the only time that matters is right now. Death teaches us a simple lesson. That is, forget about yesterday, it's over and tomorrow may never come. We haven't seen today before, so live it as well as you possibly can. Stop putting things off. The only people who should be afraid of death are those who haven't lived, those who say, 'I'll do it when I get around to it,' or 'I will tell him or her I love him or her tomorrow.' If you don't live today, your 'tomorrows' will run out. Live life now, tell people now, when their eyes are open, 'I love you.' Tomorrow it might be too late.

Remember

A little word of love and kindness during a person's life is worth far more than all the speeches after their death. Sometimes we leave it too late and we think about the many things we could have done to make someone just a little bit more happy, a little bit more loved or cared for. I notice at times at funerals how people try to outdo one another in buying the most beautiful wreath of flowers for the grave. I often think, did these people ever think of giving the person who died beautiful flowers when they were alive so they could smell the beautiful fragrance and really cherish the gift?

Don't Leave It Too Late

If ever you are going to love me, love me now while I know,

All the warm and tender feelings from real affection flow.

Love me while I am living. Don't wait till I am gone,

And then chisel it on marble ... warm love words on ice stone.

If you have dear thoughts about me, why not whisper them to me?

Surely they would make me happy and as glad as glad can be.

If you wait till I am sleeping, never more to wake again,

There'll be walls of earth between us and I cannot hear you then.

If you knew someone was thirsting for a drink of water sweet,

Would you then be slow in bringing it? Would you step with laggard feet?

There's a tender heart right near you that is thirsting for your love.

Why should you refuse to give it, since God sent it from above?

You have flowers in your garden, some are white and some are red.

Give them to me now while I am living, I can't see them when I'm dead.

I won't need your fond caresses when the grass grows over my face.

I won't want your love and kisses in my last resting place.

So if you are ever going to love me, if for just a little bit.

Won't you love me while I am living so I can treasure it?

Thought for the week

As your thought for this week, remember not to leave it until it's too late.

5

Enactment Of Charity

In life it is faith that starts us off, but it is charity that keeps us going in any undertaking in life. Little acts of charity can awaken life-giving confidence in yourself and in others.

Charity can be enacted in many ways, such as giving food and clothes to the needy, cheerful care of the sick, a warm greeting or smile to the people that you meet, or even listening to a friend's worries. As the saying goes 'Charity sees the need not the cause'.

Two very different people, Father Maximilian Kolbe and Terry Fox, enacted the term in its most challenging meaning.

Father Maximilian Kolbe

Fr Maximilian Kolbe was shipped to Auschwitz concentration camp as part of the Nazi invasion of Europe in the Second World War. In spite of the inhuman conditions, and the indignities and cruelness of camp life, he continued to carry out his priestly work.

In the summer of 1941, a prisoner escaped from his block. The penalty for escape was death by slow starvation of ten men from the same block. The next day all the men from Fr Kolbe's block had to stand to attention in the broiling sun. The Nazi officer announced, 'The fugitive has not been found, so ten of you will die in the starvation cell.' He then began to select ten men. At random the condemned were ordered to step forward. It was heartbreaking. One of the victims began to sob and started to cry, 'My poor wife and children, I will never see them again.'

Suddenly a man stepped forward from the ranks and walked directly towards the Nazi officer. 'Stop!' shouted the officer, 'What do you want?' Softly, Fr Kolbe said, 'I want to die in place of that father. I beg you to accept my offer of my life for his.'

There was a moment of silence. The Nazi officer was so dumbfounded he did not speak. He finally accepted Fr Kolbe's offer and prisoner 16670 stepped up to join the ranks of the condemned.

Terry Fox

Another person who enacted life-giving charity during his life was Terry Fox. At the age of 22, he undertook a strenuous 'Marathon of Hope' around and through Canada to raise funds for cancer research.

What made his run so special was that Terry came up with the idea for the marathon after being diagnosed with a rare form of bone cancer in1977 which required him to have most of one leg amputated.

After months of training, he began his run at Fort St John's B.C. in Thunder Bay on 12 April 1980. At first his story was given a few lines on the back pages of Canadian newspapers but by the time he had finished, he had inspired millions of people all over the world, helping to raise $24.7 million for research.

Although he was dying, Terry found the strength to do something positive and charitable for people in need. Alive with hope, he made his last year on earth a meaningful and exciting adventure. He died a national hero on 28 June 1981.

The doer of deeds

The late US President Theodore Roosevelt said:

It is not the critic that counts; not the man who points out how the strong man stumbles, or where the doer of deeds could have done better. The credit belongs to the man who is actually in the arena, whose face is marred by dust and sweat and blood; who strives valiantly; who errs, and comes short again and again, because there is no effort without error and shortcoming; who knows the great enthusiasms, the great devotions; who spends himself in a worthy cause; who at best knows in the end the triumph of high achievement. And at worst, if he fails, at least fails while daring greatly, so that his place shall never be with those cold and timid souls who know neither victory nor defeat.

Thought for the week

As your thought for this week, see what act of charity you can do or give to someone that might need it most.

6

Happiness Is ...

I have been thinking lately about what many of us in the western world define as suffering as opposed to what the people who live in developing world countries consider to be suffering, especially when you look at the serious famine in Ethiopia in 1984, the effects of the cyclone in Burma in 2008 or the earthquake in Haiti in 2010.

Of course, suffering is a very real thing in many of our lives, and it is very varied in its forms. There are many in our world who suffer from terrible poverty for example.

But sometimes it is very hard for me to understand how 'westerners', who have plenty of food, nice homes, jobs, cars and all of the things that we enjoy here, still 'suffer'. We see countless cases of broken homes, drug problems and emotional abuse, violence and murder. Many people feel at their wits end and have no place to turn.

Compassion

For us to further our journey through life, we must be able to look at the pain and the suffering of others, understand it and learn to show compassion. As we practise compassion, we are willing to look at each and every pain others have with a discerning eye and to embrace everything. The discoveries we make with our heart are never done to shame or embarrass, thus no judgments are necessary. The things we discover are there to facilitate opportunities for growth and greater understanding.

We will all face suffering and challenges in our life, some more so than others, but we will all drink from the same cup at one time or another. Our suffering allows us to become more understanding and tolerant of others who are suffering. This in turn creates a compassionate heart and a desire to reach out to others who are in pain.

It brings us in tune with others, with no consideration of backgrounds, race, religion or education levels. Suffering is something we all understand and love is the language that heals all suffering. We all have this gift to give to others through our eyes, our embrace and our words, through shared tears or a kind deed or prayer. There is no cost in compassion and many times the giver gets out of it just as much as the receiver.

The two old ladies

A beautiful, expensively dressed lady complained to her psychiatrist that her whole life was empty and had no meaning. On repeatedly hearing this, one day the doctor called over the old lady who cleaned the office floors. He said to the rich lady, 'I'm going to ask Mary here to tell you how she found happiness. All I want you to do is listen.'

So the old lady put down her broom and sat on a chair and told her story. 'Well, my husband died of malaria and three months later my only son was killed by a car. I had nobody ... I had nothing left. I couldn't sleep, I couldn't eat, I never smiled at anyone, I even thought of taking my own life. Then one evening a little kitten followed me home from work. Somehow I felt sorry for that kitten. It was cold outside, so I decided to let the kitten in. I got it some milk and it licked the plate clean. Then it purred and rubbed against my leg and for the first time in months, I smiled. Then I stopped to think; if helping a little kitten could make me smile, maybe doing something for people could make me happy. So the next day I baked some biscuits and took them to a neighbour who was sick in bed.

'From that day on, I tried to do something nice for someone every day. It made me so happy to see them happy. Today, I don't know of anybody who sleeps and eats better than I do. I've found happiness, by giving it to others.'

When she heard that, the rich lady cried. She had everything that money could buy, but she had lost the things which money cannot buy.

Thought for the week

As your thought for this week, never underestimate the power of your actions. With one small gesture you can change a person's life.

7

Making A Difference

Our world is filled with needy people, whose lives we could make a difference in if we wanted to. There are children in various parts of the world who cry out to be adopted. There are elderly people languishing in nursing homes longing for someone to talk to.

In most countries there are teenage runaways and street children. There are poor families who do not have enough to live on. In every city there are soup kitchens and charity organisations in need of food, clothes, funds and volunteers. There are men and women in prisons who would love a penpal or a visitor.

Organisations working for justice and peace always need help from willing volunteers. Political candidates trying to build a more just world always need help in getting elected. In most cities, agencies of social concern uncover any number of opportunities to help needy people.

Probably one of Jesus' most remarkable traits was his compassion for the suffering of the people just described. Jesus was extremely moved by the suffering of the poor, the sick, the dying and the socially outcast and he welcomed, healed, fed, forgave and made a difference to their lives and encouraged each of them, asking nothing in return other than that people might follow Him and help Him.

Something to offer

Everybody has something to offer. Indeed, most of us have many things to offer and, in a lot of cases, special expertise is not required. We are all capable of giving that which people need most of all: love. Love translates into time, service and the sharing of oneself.

The whole meaning of our lives is bound up with love. We find happiness in loving others and being loved in return. And all our experiences of love are experiences of God. And what really brings God's love home to us and makes it real is the love of another human being. Then we feel it and know it. After all, it is love that heals, encourages us, frees us, makes us grow and it is love alone that makes life meaningful.

You see all of us have the capacity, some more so than others, to help the needy and treat them with love, compassion and respect and show them that there are people in our world willing to help them.

Making a difference

Once upon a time there was a wise man that used to go to the ocean to do his writing. He had a habit of walking on the beach before he began his work. One day he was walking along the shore. As he looked down the beach, he saw a human figure moving like a dancer.

He smiled to think of someone who would dance to the day. So he began to walk faster to catch up. As he got closer, he saw that it was a young man and the young man wasn't dancing, but instead he was reaching down to the shore, picking up something and very gently throwing it into the ocean. As he got closer he called out, 'Good morning! What are you doing?'

The young man paused, looked up and replied, 'Throwing starfish in the ocean.'

'I guess I should have asked, why are you throwing starfish in the ocean?'

'The sun is up and the tide is going out. And if I don't throw them in they'll die.'

'But, young man, don't you realise that there are miles and miles of beach and starfish all along it. You can't possibly make a difference!'

The young man listened politely. Then bent down, picked another starfish and threw it into the sea, past the breaking waves and said, 'It made a difference for that one.'

There is something very special in each and every one of us. We have all been gifted the ability to make a difference. And if we can become aware of that gift, we gain the power to shape the future. We must each find our starfish. And if we throw our stars wisely and well, the world will be blessed.

Thought for the week

As your thought for this week, see how you can make a difference for the good in people's lives and seek out charity organisations that might need your help and support.

8

Someone's Worst Day Ever Is Someone's Best Day Ever

$\mathcal{W}$hen it comes to blessings, make no mistake about it, we are incredibly blessed, you and I.

However, life is tough. We often get caught up in the reality of our world and forget our blessings. Illness, financial woes, marital and family strife are enough to temporarily blind anyone to the blessings they enjoy. For some, it's hard to rejoice and be glad simply because their team is down by two goals in the second half of the match. On the other hand, it takes a really bad day for others to lose touch with their gladness. Still, life has a way of dealing us all with a few bad days in our life now and then.

There is an old adage that goes, 'When you're up to your rear end in alligators, it's hard to remember the objective was to drain the swamp.' Likewise, when you're overwhelmed with troubles, it's hard to follow Jesus' instructions and to 'rejoice and be glad'. I struggled with this for years and prayed for guidance. One day it came to me. There is a way for pretty much anyone to find comfort in his or her blessings at even the lowest and most difficult times. Ever since I gained this understanding, whenever I am at one of my low points, I apply this method and right away I am once again able to feel blessed and to rejoice and be glad in those blessings.

Feeling glad

The method is about perspective and not entirely unlike the old saying: 'I felt bad because I had no shoes until I met a man who had no feet.' When we are stuck in the misery of our moment, we become so consumed by it, and the troubles take on

2| 2173223

such proportion, that we become unable to see the entirety of our world. By creating contrast, things can take on a whole new look.

This is what I do. I think about Berela. Berela is 25 years old and lives in a small village outside the town of Awaza, in Ethiopia. Throughout her entire life she has known little but oppression, brutality and hunger. Not so long ago, she watched in horror as her husband and her brother were brutally beaten and killed along with others from her village.

Following the murders, she was savagely beaten then raped repeatedly by a band of thugs. There was no food and no water. In Berela's arms is her young daughter. They are both starving to death. By tomorrow her daughter could be dead and there is absolutely nothing Berela can do to prevent it.

As I focus on Berela and absorb her reality, one thing becomes incredibly clear. This may be the absolute worst day of my life, but it's also so remarkably wonderful that it's beyond Berela's ability to imagine as one of her best days ever.

My worst day is her best day ever

Think about that for a moment. For Berela and for millions of people throughout the world, in places like Darfur and Haiti, my 'worst day ever' is so good, it's beyond their ability to dare to hope for as their 'best day ever'. Whatever day Berela imagines as her 'best day ever' is pretty bleak by comparison.

No matter how awful you think things are in your life at this moment, the fact you are reading this tells me there are a lot of people in this world who can't imagine having it as good as you do right now. A few moments with Berela is all it takes to get my mind right and to help me not only know I am blessed, but to feel it to the point where I can genuinely 'rejoice and be glad'.

Thought for the week

As your thought for this week, thank God for your blessings and realise your trials can also be a blessing. Then reach out and share your gladness with someone who is struggling to find their gladness and let them know that God loves them and that within their trials are the gifts of His blessings.

9

The Man By The Window

Two men, both seriously ill, occupied the same hospital room. One man was allowed to sit up in his bed for an hour each afternoon to help drain the fluid from his lungs. His bed was next to the room's only window. The other man had to spend his time flat on his back.

The men talked for hours on end. They spoke of their wives and families, their homes, their jobs, their involvement in the army, their favourite football team, where they had been on holidays. And every afternoon when the man in the bed by the window could sit up, he would pass the time by describing to his roommate all the things he could see outside the window.

The man in the other bed began to live for those one-hour periods when his world would be broadened and enlivened by the activity and colour of the world outside. The window overlooked a park with a lovely lake. Ducks and swans played on the water while children sailed their model boats. Young lovers walked arm in arm amidst flowers of every colour of the rainbow. Grand old trees graced the landscape and a fine view of the town's skyline could be seen in the distance.

Sharing joy

As the man by the window described all this exquisite detail, the man on the other side of the room would close his eyes and imagine the picturesque scene. One warm afternoon the man by the window described a parade passing by. Although the other man couldn't hear the band, he could see it in his mind's eye as the gentleman by the window portrayed it with descriptive words.

Then, unexpectedly, a sinister thought entered his mind. Why should the other man experience all the pleasures of seeing everything while he never got to see anything? It didn't seem fair.

At first the man felt ashamed for thinking this. But, as the days passed and he missed seeing more sights, his envy eroded into resentment and soon turned him sour. He began to brood and he found himself unable to sleep. He should be by that window!

Late one night as he lay staring at the ceiling, the man by the window began to cough. He was choking on the fluid in his lungs. The other man watched in the dimly lit room as the struggling man by the window groped for the button to call for help. Listening from across the room, he never moved, never pushed his own button, which would have brought the nurse running in.

In less than five minutes, the coughing and choking stopped, and along with that, the sound of breathing. Now there was only deathly silence.

The following morning the day nurse arrived to bring water for their baths. When she found the lifeless body of the man by the window, she was saddened and called the hospital attendants to take him away.

As soon as it seemed appropriate, the other man asked if he could be moved next to the window. The nurse was happy to make the switch and, after making sure he was comfortable, she left him alone. Slowly, painfully, he propped himself up on one elbow to take his first look at the world outside. Finally, he would have the joy of seeing it all himself.

He strained to slowly turn to look out the window beside the bed. It faced a blank wall. The man asked the nurse what could have compelled his deceased roommate to describe such wonderful things that he could not see. The nurse informed him that the man by the window was blind and could not even see the wall. 'Perhaps he just wanted to encourage you,' she said.

Thought for the week

As your thought for this week, if you want to feel rich just count all of the things you have that money can't buy. Today is a gift, that's why it's called the present. There is tremendous happiness in making others happy, despite our own situation. Shared grief is half the sorrow but happiness, when shared, is doubled.

10

Time And The Thousand Marbles

*D*uring a talk I was attending recently, the lecturer asked me a rather probing question: 'What is the most precious commodity you possess?' Before I had time to answer, he shouted: 'Time!'

After thinking to myself for a while, I came to the conclusion he was right. With the gift of time, I can choose how to spend my day, I can 'give' another person time and listen to what they wish to say, or simply be with another person. By being free with my time, I can choose what is enriching and satisfying as a human being.

How do I use my time? What does it mean to me? Most of our time is used for reflections on what has happened in the past and in anticipating the future. We live between memory and expectation and we so often fail to focus on the meaning and significance of the present moment.

Focusing on the past or on the future keeps us from living in the present, from living the gift of the moment that is ours to enjoy and appreciate. And yet what is so important for us is the realisation that now, in the present, we are recreating our past and shaping our future.

The present moment is where we will meet God if we have the eyes and ears of faith to encounter the divine in the simple and humble parts of our daily lives. A story on 'time' illustrating the sacrament of the present moment might help us to reflect on how we use our time.

The thousand marbles

This story was told to me by a priest friend when I lived in Angola. It's the story about 'The Thousand Marbles' and two men, Niall and his Uncle Fearghal, having a chat about their perspectives on their own priorities in life and how Niall seems to be always caught up by his job.

'Well, Niall, it sure sounds like you're busy with your job. I'm sure they pay you well but it's a shame you have to be away from home and your family so much. Hard to believe a young fellow should have to work 60 or 70 hours a week to make ends meet. Too bad you missed your daughter's dance recital.

'Let me tell you something Niall, something that has helped me keep a good perspective on my own priorities.' And that's when Fearghal began to explain his theory of a 'thousand marbles'.

'You see, I sat down one day and did a little arithmetic. The average person lives about 75 years. Then, I multiplied 75 times 52 and I came up with 3,900, which is the number of Saturdays that the average person has in their entire lifetime. Now stick with me Niall, I'm getting to the important part.

'It took me until I was 55 years old to think about all this in any detail and, by that time, I had lived through over 2,800 Saturdays. I got to thinking that if I lived to be 75, I only had about 1,000 of them left to enjoy.

'So I went to a toy store and bought every single marble they had. I took them home and put them inside a large, clear plastic container right here in the shed next to my gear.

'Every Saturday since then, I have taken one marble out and thrown it away. I found that by watching the marbles diminish, I focused more on the really important things in life.

'There is nothing like watching your time here on this earth run out to help get your priorities straight. Now let me tell you one last thing before I sign-off with you and take my lovely wife out for breakfast. This morning, I took the very last marble out of the container. I figure if I make it until next Saturday then I have been given a little extra time. And the one thing we can all use is a little more time for one another now and then.'

Thought for the week

As your thought for this week, reflect on how you manage your time and how you share it with others. See that you use it to the benefit of yourself and others before the marbles start running out on you.

11

To Smile Is To Love

'Smiley' is the nickname I often call my wife, who is my best friend. Every time I meet her, before ever a word is spoken, I know she is glad to see me and that she cares about me. Why? Because of the beautiful radiance of her smile!

For me, one of the ways I sense God or become aware of His presence in my life is through other people. Smiling is part of that awareness. Smiles spell love, compassion, generosity, kindness, warmth, reliability, patience and real love. God's love.

God's love is not just romantic love, it's much more than that, it is a never-ending series of positive, creative, affirming, challenging, forgiving, healing and protecting feelings and actions whose purposes are to promote our sense of wellbeing for ourselves and others and helps us to be aware of how God feels lovingly and warmly towards us.

Smiles

A smile is a part of that purpose and is a powerful means of communication. It is made up, not only of parted lips but also of eyes which sparkle or weep, eyes which are full of tenderness, acceptance, humour, forgiveness, love and compassion.

Many people speak the language of smiles, especially children. I remember the smiles of orphaned and abandoned children in Africa and India and the unspoken words of love and appreciation in their smiles is a memory I will never forget.

Smiles transform the faces of all people, giving them charm, grace and a beautiful radiance. Such smiles portray the presence of love. They pour into others a portion of that love. Love changes people and it encourages them. So let us remember that love comes from God and that God's love, similarly, pours courage and strength into us.

That is why it is important to realise that God's love smiles on us. As we soak up the love of God like couples in love, we lose our absorption with self and look towards the other.

There is a saying that goes:

A smile costs nothing, but gives much. It enriches those who receive it, without making poorer those who give. It takes but a moment, but the memory of it lasts forever. It brings rest to the weary, cheer to the discouraged, sunshine to the sad and it is nature's best antidote for trouble, for it is something that is of no value to anyone until it is given away. Some people are too tired to give you a smile. Give them one of yours, as no one needs a smile so much as he who has no more to give.

Another saying or poem that my Nana Scully kept in her prayer book when she was alive reads:

Smiling is infectious, you catch it like the flu, when someone smiled at me today, I started smiling too. I passed around the corner and someone saw my grin. When he smiled, I realised I'd passed it on to him. I thought about that smile, then I realised its worth. A single smile, just like mine could travel round the earth. So, if you feel a smile begin, don't leave it undetected. Let's start an epidemic quick, and get the world infected!

Thought for the week

As your thought for this week, see what your smile does for you. You might find that you should smile more often and that the power of a smile will do wonders for you and for others.

12

True Friends Should Be Cherished

Many people will walk in and out of your life, but only true friends will leave footprints in your heart. He, who loses money, loses much; he, who loses a friend, loses much more; he, who loses faith, loses all. Beautiful young people are accidents of nature, but beautiful old people are works of art. Friends, you and me ... You brought another friend ... and we started our group ... our circle of friends ... and like a circle ... there is no beginning or end. Yesterday is history. Tomorrow is mystery. Today is a gift.

Eleanor Roosevelt (1884–1962)

True friends

True friends enrich our lives in many ways. Through a magical combination of similarities and differences, friends give us the opportunity to know ourselves as we are and help us grow into who we want to be. Our similarities attract us to each other, comforting us with familiarity when we see ourselves in them. When we are drawn to those we admire, the same recognition is at work, unconsciously acknowledging that these people possess qualities that we ourselves possess. By acting as mirrors, friends help us define who we are by reflecting ourselves back to us.

Friends also help us know ourselves through our differences. Differences allow us to see other options and make choices about who we want to be. Sometimes we are drawn to those who appear to be our opposites, and we learn to accept the parts of them we love and the parts of them that don't resonate with us, thus providing us with a valuable learning experience.

33

By expanding our understanding to include others' experiences, friends help us accept. By understanding when someone's life differs from our own, we can learn about ourselves in contrast. There are times when we see in friends what we don't like about ourselves. That mirror reflection may be hard to take, but a good friend helps us find ways we can change and supports us in that choice.

Part of the joy of friendship is the feeling that we are accepted just the way we are, with no need to change. It is a gift they give us, and one we can give back every day. Ultimately, we choose friends because they make us feel good about ourselves and life. Through tears and difficulties, friends help us find the laughter. When we find those special people who offer us that perfect combination of comfort and stimulus to grow, we are very fortunate. True friends, those wonderful companions that walk with us through life, help us define and refine who we are and who we choose to be every day.

The boy and the puppy

There is a beautiful story about friendship that involves a young boy and a puppy. A storeowner was tacking a sign above his door that read 'Puppies For Sale'. These signs had a weird way of attracting children. And sure enough, a little boy appeared at the sign. 'How much are you going to sell those puppies for?' he asked.

The store owner replied, 'Anywhere from €30 to €50.'

The little boy reached into his pocket and pulled out some change. 'I have €2.37. Can I have a look at them?'

The storeowner smiled and whistled. Out of the kennel came Pepsi, who ran down the aisle of the store followed by five teeny, tiny balls of fur. One puppy was lagging considerably behind. Immediately the little boy singled out the lagging, limping puppy and said, 'What's wrong with that little dog?'

The man explained that when the puppy was born, he had no hip socket and would limp for the rest of his life. The little boy got really excited and said, 'That's the puppy I want to buy!'

The man replied 'No, you don't want to buy that little dog. If you really want him, I'll give him to you.'

The little boy got quite upset. He looked straight into the man's eyes, and said, 'I don't want you to give him to me. He is worth every bit as much as the other dogs and I'll pay the full price. In fact, I'll give you €2.37 now and 50 cent every month until I have him paid for.'

The man countered, 'You really don't want to buy this puppy. He is never going to be able to run, jump and play like other puppies!'

To this the little boy reached down and rolled up his pant leg to reveal a badly twisted, crippled left leg, supported by a big metal brace. He looked up at the man and said, 'Well, I don't run so well myself, and the little puppy will need someone who understands.'

Thought for the week

In life, it doesn't matter who you are, but whether someone appreciates you for what you are, accepts you and loves you unconditionally. As your thought for this week, look around and be thankful and truly cherish those true friends that are part of your life.

13

Witness

I remember one of my first meetings with Mother Teresa of Calcutta. It was in her Missionaries of Charity House in Dublin. I asked her what was the secret of living a good Christian life and her answer to me was 'to be all for Jesus and to remember what Jesus said'. Using the five fingers of her right hand she said, 'You did it to me,' a summary of the quote from Matthew 25: 40-41 and indeed a summary of the entire Gospel for her.

Our job in life is to love one another and give witness to God's love and love in us. We must try to love one another as Jesus loves us. As we turn to Jesus many times in prayer, we should ask him to lead us and guide us in our own living. If we allow Jesus to enter into our living, his life will grow in us and we will want to share that life with others.

For instance, as I often do myself, when you write a letter to someone, there is a Christian way of doing it. When you speak on the phone or when you're giving advice to someone, think of God's point of view for there is also a Christian way of doing it. You give witness to God and for God when you allude to His loving presence.

Prayer in action

Prayer is often a secret or a hidden thing, like enjoying a sunset and thanking God in the process, but it can also be expressed in the way you interact with others. Prayer in action is giving witness to God's unconditional love for us. To live gladly because of the knowledge of God's love is itself a beautiful prayer. It is the way we witness God's love of us that is important. In a way we all have to be good Samaritans, so that we can hear Jesus say to us: 'You did it to me.'

One Sunday evening many moons ago, I was on the old Galway to Dublin road on my way back to college from the Midlands. There was a terrible traffic jam because of a horrible accident up ahead. There were four or five cars piled up, with other cars bashing into the pile. All but one small gap on the side of the road was completely blocked off. Traffic came to a standstill, backed up about two miles or so. I was about 15 cars back and it took over 20 minutes for all 15 cars to squeeze past the wreckage one at a time.

When I got around the wreckage, I pulled over and jumped out. People were screaming and crying, some lying bleeding on the road, one lady sticking out of the splintered side-window of her car.

When it was all over and the injured people were removed by ambulance to hospital, I wondered about the 15 cars ahead of me and the many more behind me who didn't stop.

Someone explained that people don't stop any more for fear of being asked to be a witness to the accident in court. Others fear being sued for helping someone from the wreckage. I wonder if the Good Samaritan considered the possibility of being summoned or been sued.

Thought for the week

As your thought for this week, see what opportunities there are in your life to help and support those around you that might need a helping hand. Stop and be a witness for the great unconditional love that Jesus has for each one of us and try to be a help to others whenever the opportunity arrives.

14

Feeling Good About Oneself

*O*ver the years I have come across many people who suffer from low self-esteem. What is low self-esteem you may ask?

Low self esteem makes us feel bad and disillusioned about ourselves, and, as a result, makes us withhold ourselves from other people and from activities we might enjoy and do well at. We compare ourselves unfavourably to others and envy them their good looks, jobs, personalities and friendships.

Low self-esteem usually stems from childhood deficits and damage. Our parents did not affirm or encourage us enough. Our siblings or childhood associates made fun of us or criticised us, sometimes branding us with nicknames that affected our personality and confidence. A negative self-image can also stem from failures and misfortunes that have befallen us throughout our lives, such as failed relationships, addictions, bad exam results, unemployment and failed careers.

Feeling good

God almost always supplies us with what we may not have received as small children. Friends and people come into our lives that do esteem and love us and they offer us a basis for believing more in ourselves and liking ourselves. They show us our good qualities and abilities and our possibilities.

Parents, teachers, relatives, friends are all the instruments of this gracious rebuilding action of God. The secret of life is not to focus on what we do not have but on what we do have, and to make the most of it.

We have a healing process to go through and we have an important role in it. We have to learn to have courage and belief in ourselves. We have to truly listen to the affirming, positive and loving things others say to us and really believe what they are saying to us, otherwise these words of affirmation and love make absolutely no difference.

It is important to realise that we are made happy, not only by the amount of love we give and are given, but also by the amount of love we allow ourselves to receive.

As Jesus said in Matthew's gospel: 'Love your neighbour as you love yourself.' So it is important for us to love ourselves. It's great when we can truly say: 'I love myself. I have good things and talents to share with others.'

Once we are able to do this, it does not matter whether others understand and approve everything we do or not, for we now have a positive self-image and are standing our ground.

The boy who put himself together

One lazy Sunday afternoon, a businessman was hard at work entertaining a business client at home. However, the businessman's six-year-old son, David, kept disturbing the proceedings.

David was bored. It was raining. Mum was out. His best friend had the 'flu. He hoped that Daddy and his friend might like to play a game.

But, each time David came into the room his father gave him something from the table to go away and play with. First he gave him a pen, then a calculator, then a paperweight and then a Financial Times. Finally, David was reprimanded.

A little while later David was back again, and this time, his father was prepared. On the table was a large full-colour picture of the world carefully torn into a hundred small pieces. He gave David a roll of sticky tape and asked him to play with the world until he had stuck it all back together again.

Much to his father's astonishment, David returned after about five minutes with the picture of the world complete again. 'How did you manage that so quickly, and so well?' asked his father.

David replied, 'Oh, on the back of the picture of the world I had already drawn a big picture of myself, and when I put myself together the world came together also.'

Thought for the week

As your thought for this week, acknowledge some of your special gifts and talents, and focus on all that is good and positive in your life. Thank God for loving you and creating you. It might help you to put the picture of you together.

15

God Loves Us As We Are

I often wonder why it is so difficult for people to believe that God loves us as we are. Why is it that we continue to think that God loves us only if we are perfect and go to Mass all the time and say our prayers for hours every day?

We say to ourselves, 'God couldn't possibly love me with all my faults and failings and unkept promises and lack of interest.' This can cause us to be anxious, sad and depressed instead of realising that we all make mistakes now and then.

God's love

God has loved and will continue to love us all forever, if we but allow him to. God's love for you and me embraces our whole life, every little second and particle of it. Every person is unique in God's eyes and God loves each and every person as his or her unique personal self.

The greatest thing any of us can do is to be our real self and to live our lives as lovingly and as faithfully as we can in a way that is pleasing to God. God made us for love and our whole life is a quest for love.

No matter what your standing in life, poor, rich, successful or unsuccessful, God loves you as you are, not as you would like to be. We all must be patient and gentle with ourselves and learn to accept ourselves as we are.

If we look at Holy Scriptures, we see that Jesus came to seek the lost, lonely, sick, lame, blind and those that had strayed. Why? Because he loves them and wants them to be all for him.

'It's not the healthy who need the doctor but the sick,' Jesus says. 'I have come to call not the upright, but sinners.' Jesus loves us, not despite our failures and mistakes, but because of them. His love for us is far bigger and better than we can ever think or imagine.

I think the words of the following song, 'Whenever God Shines His Light On Me', will be a fitting finale to this reflection:

Whenever God shines his light on me, opens my eyes so I can see, when I look up in the darkest night, I know everything's going to be alright. In deep confusion, in great despair, when I reach out for Him, He is there. When I am lonely, as I can be, I know God shines his light on me. He heals the sick and he heals the lame, says you can do it in Jesus' name. He'll lift you up and turn you around and put your feet on higher ground.

Thought for the week

As your thought for this week, look at the ways God shines His light in your life and be thankful for it.

16

Praying For Ice Cream

This is a story about a tidal wave of love and hope. It's about a young child's love of ice cream.

Praying for ice cream

A man was having lunch with his children in a restaurant when his young son turned to him and asked if he could say Grace. As they bowed their heads he said, 'God is great and God is good. Let us thank Him for the food, and I would even thank you more God if dad gets us ice cream for dessert! Amen!'

Along with the laughter from the other customers nearby, a woman remarked, 'That's what's wrong with this country. Kids today don't even know how to pray. Asking God for ice cream! Why, I never!'

Hearing this, the boy burst into tears and asked his dad, 'Did I do it wrong? Is God mad at me?'

The father told him he had done a terrific job and God was not mad at him. Just then an elderly gentleman approached the table. He leaned over to the child and said, 'I happen to know that God thought that was a great prayer.'

Then, in a theatrical whisper, he added (indicating the woman whose remark had started this whole thing), 'Too bad she never asks God for ice cream. A little ice cream is good for the soul sometimes.'

After lunch the father bought his children ice cream. His son stared at his for a moment. Then, without asking, he picked up his ice cream and walked over and placed it in front of the woman. With a big smile he told her, 'Here, this is for you. Ice cream is good for the soul sometimes and my soul is good already.'

Children are our hope

Young people are our source of hope and inspiration. Unfortunately, a large majority of them are being deprived of their fundamental rights and are forced to live in deplorable conditions without love, support, guidance and real care.

It is our responsibility to ensure that the nations of the world and the counties in our country value and nurture our children, for they are indeed our most precious treasure.

'If we are to have real peace, love and hope, we must
begin with the young people and the children.'

Mahatma Gandhi (1869–1948)

Thought for the week

As your thought for this week, buy somebody an ice cream who might need it. We all need a little ice cream in our lives sometimes.

17

A Little Bit Of Kindness Goes A Long Way

$\mathcal{S}$ometimes the smallest gesture can make a huge impact on someone's life. There are many different ways we can show kindness to others. A smile, a door being held open, a handwritten note, a kind word, helping someone pick up books that have fallen …

It is not the size of the action that is important, but the difference that a small action makes.

Ritchie

One day, when I was a student in secondary school, I saw a boy from my class walking home from school. His name was Ritchie. He was carrying all his books. I thought to myself, 'Why would anyone bring home all his books on a Friday? He must really be a swot.'

I had quite a weekend planned, so I shrugged my shoulders and went on. As I was walking, I saw a bunch of kids running toward him knocking all his books out of his arms and tripping him. His glasses went flying and I saw them land in the grass. He looked up and I saw this terrible sadness in his eyes. So I jogged over to him. As he crawled around looking for his glasses, I saw a tear in his eye. As I handed him his glasses, I said, 'Those guys are jerks.'

He looked at me and said, 'Hey thanks!' There was a big smile on his face that showed real gratitude. I helped him pick up his books and asked him where he lived. As it turned out, he lived near me so I asked him why I had never seen him before.

He said he had gone to private school before then. We talked all the way home and I carried his books. We hung out all weekend and the more I got to know Ritchie, the more I liked him.

Monday morning came and there was Ritchie with the huge stack of books again. I stopped him and said, 'Ritchie, you are really going to build some serious muscles with this pile of books everyday!' He just laughed and handed me half the books.

Over the next four years, Ritchie and I became best friends. When we were seniors, we began to think about college and university. Ritchie decided on UCG and I was going to Maynooth. I knew that we would always be friends, that the miles would never be a problem. He was going to be a doctor and I was going to be a teacher on a football scholarship.

As Ritchie was the head prefect of our class, he had to prepare a speech for graduation. I could see he was nervous about his speech so I smacked him on the back and said, 'Hey, big guy, you'll be great!' He looked at me and smiled.

Friendship is the best gift

Richie began his speech. 'Graduation is a time to thank those who helped you make it through those tough years: your parents, your teachers, your siblings … but mostly your friends. I am here to tell all of you that being a friend to someone is the best gift you can give him or her.'

I looked at my friend with disbelief as he told the story of the first day we met. He had planned to kill himself over the weekend. He talked of how he had cleaned out his locker. He looked hard at me and gave me a little smile.

'Thankfully, I was saved,' he said. 'My friend saved me from doing the unspeakable.' I heard the gasp go through the crowd as this handsome, popular boy told us all about his weakest moment. I saw his mum and dad looking at me and smiling that same grateful smile. Not until that moment did I realise its depth.

Thought for the week

Never underestimate the power of your actions. God puts us in each other's lives to impact on one another in some way. As your thought for this week, look for God and the good in others and remember a little kindness can go a long way!

18

The Important Things In Life

'In the world, human fulfilment is measured by material things, so that the person who has nothing is nothing.'

Laurens Van der Post (1906–1996)

People are often so preoccupied with their own concerns, they fail to hear or recognise the cries for help of the person who has nothing and is called nothing.

In our society today, people are considered important, depending on their usefulness, their social status or their authority. Their power comes from their political clout, their bank account or their ability to make themselves heard and heeded.

The Kingdom of God makes little sense against this background, for the Kingdom of God has different values. Values that are radically opposed to a world where material values are worshipped and where the unimportant are expendable!

Most of us take our lives and ourselves too seriously at times. We measure our worth by what we achieve and how successful we are in life. We tend to justify our existence by the type of people we become. People like this usually have a warped image of God, where they see him as some sort of slavemaster or taskmaster and where the important thing in life is to be useful and successful, hence the worshipping of material values and the expendability of the unimportant.

The ambitious office worker

Once there was an office worker who had a well-paid job with a thriving company. He lived with his wife and two young children in a fine house in a good neighbourhood. However, he wasn't satisfied. He was young and full of energy. Anything seemed possible. He was also full of ambition. So he said to himself, 'I can do better than this. I'll just have to work harder.'

He applied for overtime, of which there was no shortage. He doubled his salary. He moved to a larger house in a more fashionable part of town. He gave his old car to his wife and bought a sports car for himself. Even though he was doing splendidly, he was still not happy or satisfied. He had his eyes on a dream house but didn't yet have the money to buy it. But a few more years of overtime and he would.

He never did get to own that dream house, for he was struck down by a terminal illness. Suddenly he found himself at death's door. Then to his horror, he discovered that he hardly knew his children or his wife for that matter. Worse, he realised he hadn't really lived up to now. He had been postponing life until the day when all his goals would be achieved.

In the eyes of his fellow workers and of his neighbours, he was a great success. But in his own eyes he knew he had failed. He had missed out on all the important things in life. He felt empty, spiritually and emotionally. It was not the happiest state to be in now that his earthly voyage was rapidly coming to an end. He wished he could start all over again. How differently he would do things.

Thought for the week

As your thought for this week, ask yourself are you self-centred or other-centred? We need to make a shift from self-centredness to other-centredness. This is what is needed in our world today.

19

Time Of Celebration

When Brian Cowen was made Taoiseach I was asked to write a piece about 'Celebration'. I am from the same small town in Offaly as the Taoiseach.

Celebration

I found myself pondering the standard thoughts people would associate with the word 'celebration'. These included parties, people, fun, laughter, championship and election wins, gala balls/dances, song, music, drink, food and, usually, more food! Perhaps, even applause and awards. Dressing up or even dressing down. Sleeping too little, maybe even not sleeping at all! Images of people engaged in conversations with other people or even bearing witness to something very special and unique, such as one of our own being made leader of our country.

Weddings are celebrations too. A couple standing side by side at the front of a small church, filled with the excitement and trepidation of a life about to be journeyed together, with friends and family bearing witness.

A child's first birthday is a celebration I recently enjoyed. One large candle on a cake, one glowing smiling face and two small hands, along with lots of other small hands from new friends, reaching out at new things. Eyes wide, hands pulling and tugging and the expert guiding of such a large chunk of cake into such a small mouth! Presents wrapped and torn open. Flashes of light from the cameras of family and friends that capture the moment so the event can be celebrated over and over again.

Other celebrations are less noticeable. The smile from the shop attendant who gives you your daily paper. The concerned and thoughtful questions of your family doctor, your local garda or local curate. The patience of the person behind us in the queue as we sort out our financial queries with the bank assistant. The chef in the local restaurant who remembers how you like your steak or knows that you want a baby dinner and want it ready as soon as possible! Or, as I found recently, the stranger in the doctor's waiting room that entertains your energetic and restless youngster while you wait your turn.

These frequently occurring moments (if we pay attention to them and honour them) fill our hearts and touch our souls. They are moments that invite us to feel what it is to be human in our ordinary, everyday live, in the presence of another equally ordinary human being, in the creation of a magical moment, whatever you are wearing and whoever you are with.

Thought for the week

As your thought for this week, think of something important that has happened in your life, whether recently or in the past, big or small, and celebrate it with family and friends. Life is so short, it is important to make the most of every occasion.

20

Thoughts From An Oscar-Winning Movie

As the Oscars were held recently, I started thinking about an Irish Oscar-winning film. 'The Crying Game' by Neil Jordan picked up an Oscar and numerous nominations for Best Actor, Best Film and so on. But the one thing that stuck in my mind after watching that film was not the story of the film but the short story about the scorpion and the frog at the riverbank that was told by one of the main characters in the film.

The scorpion and the frog

The scorpion wanted to cross to the other side of the river, but he couldn't swim. So he called upon the frog to help him. At first the frog said no because he was afraid the scorpion would kill him. However, having received assurance from the scorpion that he wouldn't kill him, because he himself would also die as he did not know how to swim, the frog finally agreed.

The frog was about halfway across the river when the scorpion dug his poisonous tail into the frog's back, killing the frog and himself. The moral of this story is that it is in the scorpion's nature to kill.

There is a similar story involving an old man and a scorpion. The old man is trying to save the scorpion from drowning, but every time he tries to lift the scorpion from the water the scorpion stings him with his poisonous tail so badly his hands become swollen and bloody and his face becomes distorted with pain.

A passer-by sees the old man trying to save the scorpion and laughs at him. 'Only a fool would risk his life for the sake of an ugly, useless creature. Don't you know that you may kill yourself to save that ungrateful creature?' he asks.

The old man turns his head, looks straight into the stranger's eyes and replies, 'Friend, because it is the nature of the scorpion to sting and to kill, why should I give up my nature to save?'

So it is with life and nature. Lots of people in our world do not give up their nature to save us, help us and love us. No matter how many times we turn our backs on them and say no to their love or their help, they beckon to us and shower us with their love and care.

If we look at the nature of lots of our heroes and people that do good during their time on earth, we see that it was their nature to save and love and have compassion for the destitute and the dying, the sick and the sorrowful, the bereaved and the depressed.

That nature still comes to us today in many ways through the love expressed by others. For example, our parents, our friends and our neighbours who care and love us.

Thought for the week

As your thought for this week, think about the people in your life who love and care for you no matter what and be thankful for them, because we all need to be helped, loved and saved some time.

21.

Paving The Future From The Past

One thing I have noticed from my years of living in Africa and Asia is that in tribal cultures the elderly play an important role. They are the keepers of the tribe's memories and the holders of wisdom. As such, the elderly are honoured and respected members of tribes because they have paved the way for the future for their young.

Valuing the elderly

In many modern cultures, however, this is often not the case. Many elderly people say they feel ignored, left out and disrespected. This is a sad commentary on modernisation and urbanisation. It doesn't have to be this way. We can change this situation by taking the time to examine our attitudes about the elderly and taking action.

Modern societies tend to be obsessed with ideas of newness, youth and progress. Scientific studies tell us how to do everything, from the way we raise our kids to what we need to eat for breakfast. As a result, the wisdom that is passed down from older generations is often disregarded.

Of course, grandparents and retired persons have more than enough information to offer the world. Their maturity and experience allows for a larger perspective on life, and we can learn a lot from talking to elderly people. It's a shame that society doesn't do more to allow our older population to continue to feel productive for the rest of their lives.

We can all play a part in changing this. Perhaps you could help facilitate a mentorship program that would allow children to be tutored by the elderly or retirement groups. The elderly make wonderful storytellers and creating programs where they could share their real life experiences with others is another way to educate and inspire other generations.

Take stock of your relationship with the elderly population. Maybe you don't really listen to them because you hold the belief that their time has passed and they are too old to understand what you are going through. You may even realise that you don't have any relationships with older people. Try to understand why and how our cultural perception of the elderly influences the way you perceive them.

To end this thought, I want to share with you a poem or prayer I found in my Nana Scully's old prayer book. Entitled 'Wisdom', it helps me in my everyday life and it might pave the way for your future also.

> People are often unreasonable, illogical, and self-centred,
> Forgive them anyway. If you are kind, people may accuse you of selfish, ulterior motives;
> Be kind anyway. If you are successful, you will win some false friends and some true enemies;
> Succeed anyway. If you are honest and frank, people may cheat you;
> Be honest and frank anyway. What you spend years building, someone could destroy overnight;
> Build anyway. If you find serenity and happiness, they may be jealous;
> Be happy anyway. The good you do today, people will often forget tomorrow;
> Do good anyway. Give the world the best you have, and it may never be enough;
> Give the world the best you've got anyway. You see, in the final analysis,
> it is between you and God;
> It never was between you and them anyway.

Thought for the week

As your thought for this week, look around and reach out to someone who is elderly, even if you are just saying hello and making small talk. Resolve to be more aware of the elderly. They are our mothers, fathers, grandparents, family, mentors, work colleagues, wise folk and the pioneers that came before us and paved the way for our future.

22

I Want To Talk To The Manager

I have often been to Croke Park to watch hurling matches. I enjoy it and love to watch how each manager interacts with their team and how each player interacts with their manager. The better they interact with their manager, the better chance they seem to have of winning. It always reminds me of a story an Offaly hurler told me.

Talking to the manager

A stranger was walking by a local GAA pitch. He stopped to watch four kids trying to hit the sliotar over the bar. They were at the far end of the field from the stranger. The sliotar bounced to where the stranger was standing. The stranger grabbed the sliotar and let her fly. It went so high up into the air it seemed to disappear into the sky only to reappear again on its descent. The stranger was standing at least 120 yards away from the goal. The sliotar went straight over the black spot of the goal. The kids went wild roaring 'no way!' and 'lucky shot'. The stranger yelled out, 'One more shot!' to which one kid replied, 'Ain't no way he can do two. The wind is blowing.'

One of the kids hit the sliotar down to where the stranger was standing. He let her fly again. This time, everything got quiet even though the wind still blew as hard as ever. The sliotar again went straight over the black spot. The kids were stunned.

One kid hit the sliotar toward the stranger again. The stranger lofted the sliotar up in the air the same way with the same result. 'You boys want to learn how to be top hurlers?' he called out as he drew closer.

One kid asked, 'Who are you man?'

The stranger said, 'I'm just passing through. Want to learn how to hurl? I'll show you how.'

The stranger worked with each kid showing him how to improve his hurling. Every kid improved immediately. It got so the kids couldn't miss.

Suddenly, the stranger disappeared. Three of the four boys looked around and saw only an empty green field. The other kid's mouth had dropped wide open. He was frozen in place. They were sure they had seen a ghost.

Suddenly the stranger reappeared out of thin air. 'I am not a ghost. I do what the manager tells me to do. Today I am a teacher, teaching you how to play hurling and other things about life. I taught you how to hurl but I also taught you about more important things than hurling. Remember I taught you if you don't have a goal, you don't have a game. I taught you unless you pass the sliotar and share the scoring you lose. I taught you if you do not follow the rules, you cannot win. I taught you that you have to be honest with yourself. You need to know what you can and cannot do. I taught you to develop the part of your game you do best. I taught you to play defence against the bad things of life and play attacking to keep the good things going. I taught you to improve your game and improve your character. I taught you not to repeat mistakes in your game but to eliminate the mistakes as soon as you can. You must quickly eliminate the mistakes, so the mistakes do not become a habit. I taught you to put others before yourself.

'One more thing, you must always talk to the manager. If you don't talk to the manager, the manager won't talk to you,' he said before disappearing again.

The boys froze. One kid said, 'I think my mother sent this guy.'

Another kid said, 'No, your mother wouldn't send a strange guy to teach us to play hurling. She'd send Brian Whelahan, or Joe Connolly, or DJ Carey, or some other famous hurling star.'

They all kind of laughed but the kid persisted and said, 'No man, my mother is always praying for me. My mother is always talking to the manager.'

Thought for the week

As your thought for this week, see where you need help from your manager. Listen to what he is telling you and try your best to get a good result.

23

The Girl With The Rose

$\mathcal{O}$ften in our lives we fall prey to the idea of a thing rather than actually experiencing the thing itself. We see this at play in our love lives and in the love lives of our friends and our family.

Real love is identifiable by the way it makes us feel. Love should feel good. An authentic experience of love does not ask us to look a certain way, drive a certain car or have a certain job. It takes us as we are.

The girl with the rose

John O'Grady stood up from the bench, straightened his army uniform and studied the crowd of people making their way through Heuston Station. He looked for the girl whose heart he knew, but whose face he didn't: the girl with the rose.

John's interest in the girl with the rose began 13 months earlier in a Galway library. Taking a book from a shelf, he found himself intrigued not with the words on the page but with the notes pencilled in the margin. The soft handwriting reflected a thoughtful soul and insightful mind. In the front of the book, he discovered the previous owner's name, Miss Hollis Maynell. With time and effort, he located her address. She lived in Dublin City. He wrote her a letter inviting her to correspond. The next day he was shipped overseas for service in World War II.

Over the course of the next year, the two grew to know each other. Each letter was a seed falling on a fertile heart. A romance was budding. O'Grady requested a photograph, but she refused. If he really cared, it shouldn't matter what she looked like. When the day finally came for him to return from Europe, they scheduled their first meeting: 7 pm at Heuston Station in Dublin.

'You'll recognise me,' she wrote, 'by the red rose I'll be wearing on my lapel.' So at 7 pm, he was in the station looking for a girl whose heart he loved, but whose face he'd never seen. I'll let Mr O'Grady tell you what happened.

'A young woman was coming toward me, her figure long and slim. Her blonde hair lay back in curls from her delicate ears; her eyes were blue as flowers. Her lips and chin had a gentle firmness, and in her pale green suit she was like springtime come alive. I started toward her, entirely forgetting to notice that she was not wearing a rose. As I moved, a small, provocative smile curved her lips. "Going my way, sailor?" she asked. Almost uncontrollably I made one step closer to her, and then I saw Hollis Maynell.

'She was standing almost directly behind the girl. A woman well past 40, she had greying hair tucked under a worn hat. She was more than plump, her thick-ankled feet thrust into low-heeled shoes. The girl in the green suit was walking quickly away. I felt as though I was split in two, so keen was my desire to follow her, and yet so deep was my longing for the woman whose spirit had truly companioned me. And there she stood. Her pale, plump face was gentle and her grey eyes had a warm and kindly twinkle.

'I did not hesitate. My fingers gripped the small worn blue leather copy of the book that was to identify me to her. This would not be love, but it would be something precious, something perhaps even better than love, a friendship for which I had been and must ever be grateful.

'I squared my shoulders and saluted and held out the book to the woman, even though while I spoke I felt choked by my disappointment. "I'm Lieutenant John O'Grady and you must be Miss Maynell. I am so glad you could meet me; may I take you to dinner?"

The woman's face broadened into a tolerant smile. "I don't know what this is about, son," she answered, "but the young lady in the green suit who just went by, she begged me to wear this rose on my coat. And she said if you were to ask me out to dinner, I should go and tell you that she is waiting for you in the big restaurant across the street. She said it was some kind of test!"'

Thought for the week

As your thought for this week, take a moment to feel and see love just as it is all around you and within you.

24

To My Child

When I was in Ethiopia adopting our little girl, I saw much tragedy, sadness and suffering. The people, especially the children, need plenty of help and support. However, while they may be poor, they are the most welcoming and friendly people I have ever met. At times I came away feeling it was me who had been helped, not them.

Gita

My thoughts go back to Gita, a beautiful young girl, who, at two years of age, is living with HIV/AIDS. Since the death of her mother from the same disease, she is being looked after by the nuns in the orphanage. She is beautiful and has a face like an angel. I just wonder if she will still be around on my next visit.

To live without hope is the most crushing of all burdens. Everywhere I went on my trip to Ethiopia, and indeed in many of the famine areas of the rural regions, I saw children with a look of despair. I was reminded of the words of the American writer James Agee who said that: 'In every child who is born, under no matter what circumstances, the potentiality of the human race is born again, and in them too, once more and in each of us, is born again our terrific responsibility towards human life.'

I hug my little daughter tightly each day and thank God for the beautiful Ethiopian angel he has given us. I remember the poem called 'To My Child' on the wall of a children's hospice:

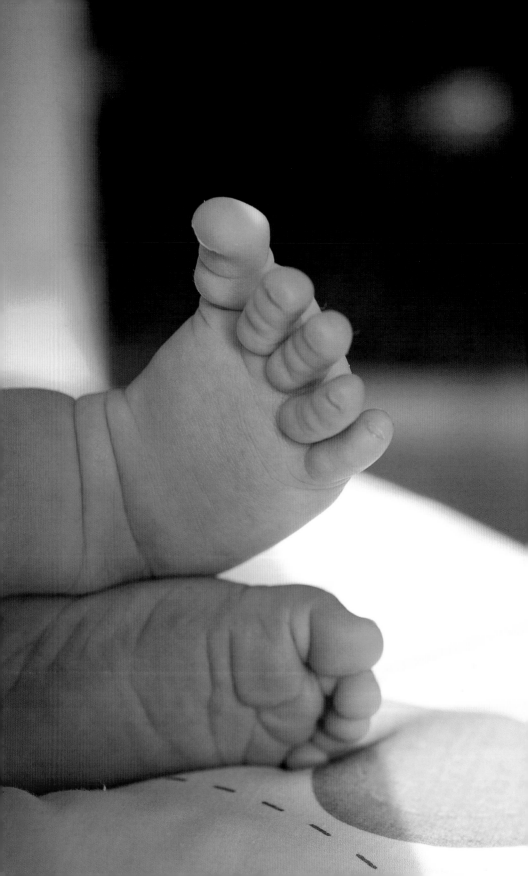

Just for this morning, I am going to smile when I see your face and laugh when I feel like crying.

Just for this morning, I will let you choose what you want to wear, and smile and say how perfect it is.

Just for this morning, I am going to step over the laundry, and pick you up and take you to the park to play.

Just for this morning, I will leave the dishes in the sink, and let you teach me how to put that puzzle of yours together.

Just for this afternoon, I will unplug the telephone and keep the computer off, and sit with you in the backyard and blow bubbles.

Just for this afternoon, I will not yell once, not even a tiny grumble when you scream and whine for the ice cream truck, and I will buy you one if he comes by.

Just for this afternoon, I won't worry about what you are going to be when you grow up, or second guess every decision I have made where you are concerned.

Just for this afternoon, I will let you help me bake cakes, and I won't stand over you trying to fix them.

Just for this afternoon, I will take us to Supermacs and buy us both a Supermacs' meal so we can have both toys.

Just for this evening, I will hold you in my arms and tell you a story about how you were born and how much I love you.

Just for this evening, I will let you splash in the tub and not get angry.

Just for this evening, I will let you stay up late while we sit on the porch and count all the stars.

Just for this evening, I will snuggle beside you for hours, and miss my favourite TV shows.

Just for this evening, when I run my finger through your hair as you pray, I will simply be grateful that God has given me the greatest gift ever given.

I will think about the mothers and fathers who are searching for their missing children, the mothers and fathers who are visiting their children's graves instead of their bedrooms, and mothers and fathers who are in hospital rooms watching their children suffer senselessly, and screaming inside that they can't handle it anymore. And when I kiss you good night, I will hold you a little tighter, a little longer. It is then that I will thank God for you, and ask him for nothing, except one more day ...

Thought for the week

As your thought for this week, do something special with your loved ones, especially your children.

25

Wishing For Peace In Our World

One of my most abiding wishes is that we all live in peace together. We have seen what peace can do for people in Northern Ireland. But you only have to watch the news or read the papers to find conflict and suffering in every corner of the world.

The causes may seem complex, but I believe the root of much of it is one group trying to impose its will on another. The motives may be political, religious or racial arrogance, but it amounts to the same thing. One group sees itself as 'right' and others as 'wrong'. Religion and politics are often used to justify such claims.

Agree to disagree

It seems to me that the only way we will ever achieve a peaceful world is if we resist the urge to impose our beliefs on someone who does not want to share them. We must accept everyone's right to follow their own path.

Accept that there will always be those who hold different beliefs and follow different paths to our own. Learn to respect people as they are and put differences aside. Agree to disagree.

This does not mean we cannot state our views. But it does mean I will not impose anything on anyone who is not interested and it means that I can accept, respect and share with those who hold different beliefs from me without feeling the need to impose my ideas upon them.

The King

There once was a King who offered a prize to the artist who would paint the best picture of peace.

When the entries were in, the King looked at all the pictures. There were only two he really liked. One picture was of a calm lake. The lake was a perfect mirror, with four peaceful towering mountains all around it. Overhead was a blue sky with fluffy white clouds. All who saw this picture thought that it was a perfect picture of peace.

The other picture had mountains too, but these were rugged and bare. Above was an angry sky from which rain fell and lightening played. Down the side of the mountain tumbled a foaming waterfall. It did not look peaceful at all.

However, when the King looked, he saw a tiny bush growing in a crack in the rock behind the waterfall. In the bush a mother bird had built her nest. There, in the midst of the rush of angry water, sat the mother bird on her nest, perfectly at peace.

The King chose the second picture because, he said, 'Peace does not mean to be in a place where there is no noise, trouble or hard work. Peace means to be in the midst of all those things and still be calm in your heart. That is the real meaning of peace.'

We often look at the outside world and find it in a state of chaos and disorder. We cannot bring to the world that which we do not have to offer. Peace starts in our own minds and hearts, and until its roots are firmly entrenched in our own selves, we cannot manifest it externally.

As Eleanor Roosevelt said, 'It isn't enough to talk about peace. One must believe in it. And it isn't enough to believe in it. One must work at it.'

Thought for the week

As your thought for this week, look at ways you can bring real, lasting and genuine peace into your life and the lives of those around you.

26

A Story Of Discovery And Rediscovering

The first thing I did each day during my time working on the streets of Calcutta in India was walk to the convent of Mother Teresa. I attended mass before heading out on the streets where I worked with street children, child labourers, the lepers and the dying.

At one of these masses an Indian priest gave a beautiful sermon. He told a story about a family and their joy of discovering and rediscovering.

The child and the toy

One day a child got the toy he had longed for. He had seen it advertised and it was the most sought after toy ever. He hugged it as if it was priceless and readily agreed with his parents who told him that, as it was very expensive, they would not be able to afford another toy for him.

He called his friends and showed them his new toy with satisfaction. But the elation did not last long. After a few weeks, one of his friends got the latest toy available, the one that was now the most sought after toy.

The child lost interest in his toy and though his mother tried to explain that his toy was a very good one, he looked away and sulked. The toy, now rejected, remained forgotten in a corner.

The child's mother had her own problems. After much planning and saving, she had just gotten her new home and was working hard to ensure it would be the pride of the community. This was until a new house was built in the community.

When it was completed, the new house was undoubtedly the most modern house in the community. The owner invited her around and showed her inside. When she went back to her own house, she looked at it anew and her heart sank. The house looked common and was not worth any attention or special care.

From that moment on, she lost interest in her own home. She stopped taking the trouble to clean the house and it became dirty. Her husband noticed the change in the home and in his wife and gently inquired. His wife told him she was no longer interested in the house because the neighbour's house was better. He tried to explain to her that their house was fine and was better that most houses. But the woman remained silent and sulked.

The woman's husband had personal problems too. His wife was beautiful and he was madly in love with her but his friends had young wives and some of them were very beautiful. As he came to know them, his interest in his wife diminished and his feelings changed. A growing coldness crept between them. His wife tried to talk to him, but he remained silent.

One day the child's eye fell on the old abandoned toy. He started playing with it contentedly. He had not noticed that the door of his room was slightly ajar and his mother was looking at him with loving curiosity. She felt happy in her heart that her child had made friends again with his old toy, and she smiled to herself in silence.

The next day, as she was sitting alone in her home, she noticed how dusty and dirty it was. She rose to her feet and began tidying the house. She had rediscovered her interest in her house and once more she became the efficient housewife she used to be.

As her husband approached the house, he noticed his wife going enthusiastically about her chores and at once rejoiced. He felt happy that his wife had reconciled herself with the house and he smiled to himself in silence.

The next day, when the husband and wife were seated in their sitting room, the husband looked at his wife and suddenly realised again what a beautiful woman she was. In that moment, he realised he loved her more than ever. He went to her and took her in his arms.

Thought for the week

As your thought for this week, rediscover the good in your life. Cherish it and hold on to it.

27

Trading Places With The Working Mother

'Help, I'm a working mother!' I hear it all the time. It's a common cry and one so many women understand. If you are a mother, by definition you are a working mother. You don't have to collect a salary; all you have to have is someone who calls you 'mum', relies on you, needs you and is in your care somehow.

Reality for many working mothers is having too much to do and not enough time to do it. I remember my mother trying to work outside the home, getting up early, getting babies and school-age children ready for school, while trying to get herself ready for the working day.

Setting the tone

They say the first half hour of the day sets the tone for the rest of the day. If so, my mother's tone was set at stress and anger before she left the house. She then had to go to work and deal with the pressure and demands of the workplace, trying to perform her duties, while thinking about and missing her children. At the end of the workday, the home workday would just begin: helping us kids get homework started, getting dinner ready, then washing the dishes, getting the laundry started, refereeing fights …

Add to the fun, time with my dad, relationships with family and friends, grocery shopping, paying bills, doctor and dentist appointments, illnesses, bringing us to and from sporting or after school events and the result was often one tired, burned out mother. Even going into the bathroom as a safe haven of solitude and silence did not work; we always found her. From what I can see from my mother and my wife, being a mum can often be very tiring and lonely. Mums often feel isolated and defeated, and wonder if there is any relief. Fortunately, there is.

Remember, this is only one season. Children will grow up and become independent all too soon. While in the midst of the season, it is vital to take some time for yourself and to ask God in prayer or meditation for help and guidance. It's amazing what God can and will do to help you through those times when you believe you can't go one more step or do one more thing. A story might help.

Trading Places

A man was sick and tired of going to work every day while his wife stayed home. He wanted her to see what he went through. He prayed to God: 'Dear Lord, I go to work every day and put in eight hours while my wife merely stays at home. I want her to know what I go through, so please allow her body to switch with mine for a day.'

God, in his infinite wisdom, granted the man's wish. The next morning, he awoke as a woman. He got up, cooked breakfast for his wife, woke the kids, got them dressed for school, fed them breakfast, packed their lunches and drove them to school. He then picked up the laundry, stopped at the bank to make a payment and went food shopping, before driving home to put away the groceries, pay the bills and balance the accounts. He cleaned the cat's litter box and washed the dog. It was already lunchtime. He hurried to make the beds, do the cleaning and mop the kitchen floor. He ran to the school to pick up the kids, getting into an argument with them on the way home.

Setting out a drink and a snack, he got the kids to do their homework, while he set up the ironing board. At 4.30 pm, he began peeling spuds and washing vegetables for dinner. He breaded the pork chops and snapped fresh beans. After dinner, he cleaned the kitchen, ran the dishwasher, folded clothes, washed the kids, and put them to bed. At 9 pm, he was wrecked.

The next morning he awoke and immediately knelt by the bed and said, 'Lord, I don't know what I was thinking. I was so wrong to envy my wife. Please, oh please, let us trade back.'

The Lord, in his infinite wisdom, replied, 'My son, I feel you have learned your lesson and I will be happy to change things back to the way they were. You'll just have to wait nine months, though. You got pregnant last night.'

Thought for the week

As your thought for this week, try to empathise with those close to you and, at times of stress in their lives, try to see things from their point of view.

28

Making It On Your Own

Nowadays it is fashionable to think of oneself first. In relationships, we are urged to make others happy by making ourselves happy. Our careers, our interests and our personal ambitions are a priority. With self-centredness the norm, selfless ideas no longer command widespread lip service, let alone respect. We view sacrifice as a sign of weakness.

Yet sacrifice remains central to human evolution. No matter where we are or what we are doing, we have the choice of dedicating our efforts to helping others or exalting ourselves. As usual, a story might help to illustrate what I am saying about real sacrifice for the good of another in our lives.

The praying hands

Back in the fifteenth century, in a tiny village near Nuremberg, lived a family with 18 children. In order to keep food on the table, the father, a goldsmith by profession, worked almost 18 hours a day at his trade and any other paying chore he could find in the neighbourhood. Despite their seemingly hopeless conditions, two of Albrecht Durer the Elder's children had a dream: they wanted to pursue their talent for art. However, they knew their father could never afford to send either of them to Nuremberg to study at the academy. After many long discussions at night, the two boys finally worked out a pact. They would toss a coin. The loser would go down into the nearby mines and, with his earnings, support his brother while he attended the academy. Then, when that brother who won the toss completed his studies, he would support the other brother at the academy, either with sales of his artwork or, if necessary, also by labouring in the mines. They tossed a coin on a Sunday morning after church. Albrecht Durer won the toss and went off to Nuremberg.

His brother Albert went down into the dangerous mines and, for the next four years, financed his brother, whose work at the academy was almost an immediate sensation. Albrecht's etchings, his woodcuts and his oils were far better than those of most of his professors and by the time he graduated he was beginning to earn considerable fees for his commissioned works. When the young artist returned to his village, the Durer family held a festive dinner on their lawn to celebrate Albrecht's triumphant homecoming. After a long and memorable meal, punctuated with music and laughter, Albrecht rose from his honoured position at the head of the table to drink a toast to his beloved brother for the years of sacrifice that had enabled Albrecht to fulfil his ambition. His closing words were: 'And now, Albert, blessed brother of mine, it is your turn. Now you can go to Nuremberg to pursue your dream, and I will take care of you.'

All heads turned in eager expectation to the far end of the table where Albert sat, tears streaming down his face, shaking his lowered head from side to side. 'No ... no ... no,' he sobbed. Finally, Albert rose and wiped the tears from his cheeks. He glanced down the long table at the faces he loved. Holding his hands close to his right cheek, he said softly, 'No, brother. I cannot go to Nuremberg. It is too late for me. Look what four years in the mines have done to my hands! The bones in every finger have been smashed at least once, and lately I have been suffering from arthritis so badly in my right hand that I cannot even hold a glass to return your toast, much less make delicate lines on parchment or canvas with a pen or a brush. No, brother ... for me, it is too late.'

More than 450 years have passed. By now, Albrecht Durer's hundreds of masterful portraits, pen and silver point sketches, water-colours, charcoals, woodcuts and copper engravings hang in every great museum in the world.

Of course, most of us are only familiar with one of Albrecht Durer's works. Indeed, many of us will have a reproduction of it hanging in our homes or offices. To pay homage to Albert for all he had sacrificed, Albrecht Durer painstakingly drew his brother's abused hands with palms together and thin fingers stretched skyward. He called his powerful drawing simply 'Hands' but it has become popularly known as 'The Praying Hands'.

Thought for the week

As your thought for this week, the next time you see a copy of that touching creation 'The Praying Hands', take a second look. Let it be your reminder, if you still need one, that no one ever makes it alone!

29

The Potter's Hand

On a recent trip to Galway, I stopped into Judy Green's pottery shop. I love looking at the way she moulds shapes out of clay.

In the book of Isaiah, the prophet says, 'O Lord, you are our father; we are the clay, and you our potter; and we all are the work of your hand.' We can learn something from simple clay. In its natural state, clay is common and far from beautiful. But in the hands of a master potter like Judy Green, it takes on a pleasing personality, becoming a thing both of usefulness and unique beauty.

Sometimes flaws appear in the clay and repairs must be made. It may be necessary to go back, to remould and reshape. The wonderful thing is, when properly repaired, the flaw is completely gone, as though it had never existed.

When we sin, we introduce flaws and defects. They may not be outwardly visible at first, but they weaken us just the same. And if they are not properly repaired, they can lead to our ultimate ruin. Fortunately, if we are humble and pliable as clay in the potter's hands, repentance will make us completely whole.

There is a story I heard from a Christian brother in Calcutta that might help in explaining what I am writing about.

The cracked pot

A water bearer had two large pots. They hung on each end of a pole that he carried across his neck. One of the pots had a crack in it and, while the other pot was perfect and always delivered a full portion of water at the end of the long walk from the stream to the master's house, the cracked pot arrived only half full.

For a full two years this went on daily, with the bearer delivering only one and a half pots full of water to his master's house. The perfect pot was proud of its accomplishments but the poor cracked pot was ashamed of its imperfection and miserable that it was able to accomplish only half of what it had been made to do. After two years of what it perceived to be a bitter failure, it spoke to the water bearer one day by the stream.

'I am ashamed of myself and I want to apologise to you,' it said.

'Why?' asked the bearer. 'What are you ashamed of?'

'I have been able, for these past two years, to deliver only half my load because this crack in my side causes water to leak out all the way back to your master's house. Because of my flaws, you have to do all of this work and you don't get full value from your efforts,' the pot said.

The water bearer felt sorry for the old cracked pot and in his compassion he said, 'As we return to the master's house, I want you to notice the beautiful flowers along the path.'

Indeed, as they went up the hill, the old cracked pot took notice of the sun warming the beautiful wild flowers on the side of the path. This cheered it some. But at the end of the trail, it still felt bad because, again, it had leaked out half its load.

The water bearer asked the pot, 'Did you notice that there were flowers only on your side of your path, but not on the other pot's side? That's because I have always known about your flaw and I took advantage of it.

'I planted flower seeds on your side of the path and every day while we walk back from the stream, you've watered them. For two years, I have been able to pick these beautiful flowers to decorate my master's table. Without you being just the way you are, he would not have this beauty to grace his house.'

We're all cracked pots, but if we allow it, the Lord will use our flaws to grace His Father's table. In God's great economy, nothing goes to waste.

Thought for the week

As your thought for this week, look at the flaws in your life and ask your potter to remould them and make them new again, so that you can bring beauty into people's lives.

30

The Littlest Policeman's Last Wish

$\mathcal{T}$his touching story is extra special because it's true. It's a story about a little boy who became the very first child to benefit from one of the most famous children's charities. He became known as 'The Littlest Policeman in the World'. It demonstrates the good that charities do and how they inspire change.

Bopsy

A 26-year-old mother stared down at her son who was living with the life- threatening illness leukaemia. Although her heart was filled with sadness, she was determined. Like any parent, she wanted her son to grow up and fulfil his dreams. However, that was no longer possible.

Still, she wanted her son's dreams to come true. She took his hand and asked, 'Bopsy, did you ever think about what you wanted to be once you grew up? Did you ever dream and wish what you would do with your life?'

'Mommy, I always wanted to be a policeman when I grew up,' Bopsy replied. His mom smiled back and said, 'Let's see if we can make your wish come true.'

Later that day, she went to her local police department in Phoenix, Arizona, where she met policeman Bob, who had a heart as big as Phoenix. She explained her son's final wish and asked if it might be possible to give her six-year-old son a ride around the block in the police car.

'Look, we can do better than that,' policeman Bob said. 'If you'll have your son ready at seven o'clock Wednesday morning, we'll make him an honorary policeman for the whole day. He can come down to the police station, eat with us, go out on all the calls, the whole nine yards! And if you'll give us his sizes, we'll get a real police uniform for him with a real hat, not a toy one, with the emblem of the Phoenix Police Department on it. They're all manufactured right here in Phoenix so we can get them fast.'

Three days later policeman Bob picked Bopsy up, dressed him in his police uniform and escorted him from his hospital bed to the waiting police truck. Bopsy was in heaven. There were three calls in Phoenix that day and he got to go out on all three. He rode in the different police engines, the paramedic's van, even the chief's car. He was also videotaped for the local news programme. Having his dream come true, with all the love and attention that was lavished upon him, deeply touched Bopsy. He lived three months longer than any doctor thought possible.

However, one night in the hospital months later, all of Bopsy's vital signs began to drop dramatically and the head nurse began to call the family members to the hospital.

She remembered the day Bopsy spent as a policeman, so she called the police chief and asked if it would be possible to send a uniformed policeman to the hospital to be with Bopsy as he made his transition.

'We can do better than that,' the chief replied. 'We'll be there in five minutes. Will you please do me a favour? When you hear the sirens screaming and see the lights flashing, will you announce over the PA system that there is not an incident? It's just the police department coming to see one of its finest members one more time. And will you open the window to his room?'

Five minutes later, police cars arrived at the hospital and the policemen made their way up to Bopsy's third floor. With his mother's permission, they hugged him and held him and told him how much they loved him.

With his dying breath, Bopsy looked up at the chief and asked, 'Chief, am I really a policeman now?'

'Yes, Bopsy, you are a policeman now,' the chief said. With those words, Bopsy smiled and closed his eyes one last time. He passed away later that evening.

Thought for the week

As your thought for this week, remember how precious life is, and how special the moment of death can be. Also, remember the good that charitable organisations do.

31

Where Your Treasure Is...

'Where your treasure is, there will your heart be also.' Not a quote from former RTÉ economics editor George Lee or *The Sunday Business Post's* David McWilliams, but from Matthew 6:21. It is the gospel quote that challenges us to see that wealth is not about material possessions, it's about depth of relationship. Likewise, true progress is not just about economic growth, it's about the development of the human person.

Where our treasure is

'Where your treasure is, there will your heart be also', to my mind, led to an encyclical, *Populorum Progressio* (On The Development Of Peoples), published 40 years or so ago by Pope Paul VI. It came in response to the poverty and injustice he saw in the world and his feeling that the world's economy should serve mankind, not just the few.

It is a prophetic document, penetrating to the heart of the human predicament at the moment with the world's monetary markets in turmoil. It questions how we can develop as a people in a way that is fair for all. While globalisation has made our world smaller, our neighbours are, ironically, no closer. Moreover, the gulf that exists between those who have more than enough and those who have less than they need has widened.

'Where your treasure is, there will your heart be also' has justice at its heart. It charges us to take seriously our place as stewards of God's creation for the sake of future generations, and highlights the need for promoting trade justice, as well as the necessity of mutual solidarity between donor and recipient when it comes to aid and debt relief.

If we walk away from the call to live in solidarity with the poor we choose the path to self-destruction. More than ever, the earth urgently needs our nurture, our neighbours need our understanding, and we ourselves need tending.

Asking questions

Begin by asking yourself three basic questions: what part of my life is cluttered; what part of my life is depleted; and what part of my life is closed?

Perhaps our lives are cluttered by too many possessions, or too much work. If so, work out ways to live in a more just manner. Look at why we work so hard. Is it to avoid spending time with our partner, or does it stem from peer pressure, an unreasonable workload or greed?

We could take steps to deal with the underlying cause. Too much clutter may be compensating for areas in our lives that are depleted. Perhaps we are subconsciously yearning for something more, the spiritual treasure that money can't buy.

Living sustainably is about more than recycling. It is about our emerging transformation. Just as our environment needs to be cherished, we need to be nourished. Make time to pray and reflect, to listen to the still small voice and to the breathing of God's earth. Allow the seeds of change to germinate.

Perhaps we could walk more and drive less. Be aware of the water we use and the electricity we can save. Recycle and recreate. Turn off the television and have a conversation. We can't live on empty, and neither can the earth.

Perhaps a part of your life is closed. Let's begin by asking ourselves how we view difference, and whether we are open to people of other faiths and cultures. Do we welcome the asylum-seeker or refugee? Are we interested in the lives of the people who have picked our tea, or who beg in the streets? Living in solidarity with people who are poor means finding out about their lives, listening to their hopes and fears, and understanding their yearning for God's Kingdom.

So let's open our eyes and ears, and not least our hearts. If we each took one small step to live just and sustainable lives in solidarity with people who are poor, it would be one giant leap for humankind.

Thought for the week

As your thought for this week, look at ways you can help create a world in which human dignity is respected and where everyone can reach their full potential. This would be true progress, worth more than any economic growth alone.

32

Kindness Pays

Abraham Lincoln once said:

Kindness is the only service that will stand the storm of life and not wash out. It will wear well and be remembered long after the prism of politeness or the complexion of courtesy has faded away. When I am gone, I hope it can be said of me that I plucked a thistle and planted a flower wherever I thought a flower would grow.

In the quest to create a gentler, more loving world, kindness is the easiest tool we can use. Though it is easy to overlook opportunities to be kind, our lives are full of situations in which we can be helpful, considerate, thoughtful and friendly to loved ones and colleagues, as well as strangers. The touching, selfless acts of kindness that have the most profoundly uplifting effects are often the simplest: a word of praise, a gentle touch, a helping hand, a gesture of courtesy, or a smile.

Such small kindnesses represent an unconditional, unrestricted form of love that we are free to give or withhold at will. When you give the gift of kindness, whether in the form of assistance, concern, or friendliness, your actions create a beacon of happiness and hope that warms people's hearts. The components of kindness are compassion, respect and generosity. Put simply, kindness is the conscious act of engaging others in a positive way without asking whether those individuals deserve to be treated kindly.

All living beings thrive on kindness. A single, sincere compliment can turn a person's entire world around. Holding a door, or thanking someone who has held a door for you, can inspire others to practise politeness and make already kind individuals feel good about their efforts. Smiling at people you meet, even those who make you feel like frowning, can turn a dreary encounter into a delightful one, for both of you. Every kind act has a positive influence on the individual who has performed the act as well as on the recipient, regardless of whether the act is acknowledged. Kindness brings about more kindness and slowly but surely makes a positive impact on humanity.

Weaving the thread of kindness into your everyday life can be as easy as choosing to offer a hearty 'good morning' and 'good night' to your co-workers or neighbours, a stranger on the street, or the shop assistant.

When you commit a kind act, you are momentarily disconnected from your ego and bonded with the individual who has benefited from your kindness. Being fully present in each moment of your life facilitates kindness as it increases your awareness of the people around you. You'll discover that each act of kindness you engage in makes the world, in some small way, a better place.

The benefits of kindness

One day, a poor boy who was selling goods from door to door to pay his way through school, found he had only one thin cent left and he was hungry. He decided he would ask for a meal at the next house. However, he lost his nerve when a lovely young woman opened the door. Instead of a meal he asked for a drink of water. She thought he looked hungry so brought him a large glass of milk. He drank it slowly, and then asked, 'How much do I owe you?'

'You don't owe me anything,' she replied 'Mother has taught us never to accept payment for a kindness.'

He said, 'Then I thank you from my heart.' As Howard Kelly left that house, he not only felt stronger physically, but his faith in God and man was strong also. He had been ready to give up and quit.

Years later that young woman became critically ill. The local doctors were baffled. They finally sent her to the big city where they called in specialists to study her rare disease. Dr. Howard Kelly was called in for the consultation. When he heard the name of the town she came from, a strange light filled his eyes. Immediately he rose and went down the hall of the hospital to her room. Dressed in his doctor's gown he went in to see her. He recognised her at once. He went back to the consultation room determined to do his best to save her life. From that day he gave special attention to the case.

After a long struggle, the battle was won. Dr Kelly requested the business office to pass the final bill to him for approval. He looked at it, then wrote something on the edge and the bill was sent to her room. She feared to open it, for she was sure it would take the rest of her life to pay for it all. Finally, she looked and something caught her attention on the side as she read these words: 'Paid in full with one glass of milk.' (Signed) Dr Howard Kelly.

Tears of joy flooded her eyes as her happy heart prayed: 'Thank you God, that your love has spread abroad through human hearts and hands.'

Thought for the week

As your thought for the week, practice genuine kindness as much as you can in your daily life and plant flowers wherever you can!

33

An Attitude of Gratitude

For many, the last few years has been a rollercoaster. And some are ready to get off the ride! The economy has impacted everyone, some more than others. And the impact hasn't just been financial. Attitudes, emotions, plans and mindsets have all been affected. The recession and the floods have resulted in a culture-wide increase in stress and anxiety. The Christmas season is a time that is anticipated with both joy and anxiety. Sure, we love the celebrations, the family traditions, and we cherish the memories of holidays gone by; but along with them, we add the stresses of preparation, expectations and the fear of letdowns or family squabbles that we have experienced in the past. And this year, the stress and anxiety level is likely to be amplified because of the year we just had. With this in mind, here are a few tips I believe can be helpful in getting ready for an enjoyable, meaningful Christmas season.

Helpful tips for a meaningful Christmas season

Try to set manageable expectations. Spend some time setting realistic expectations for your Christmas. Understand that you can't do everything and with our current economic realities you might not be able to do everything you've done in the past. So, be realistic about what you can do. Remember that Christmas does not eliminate sadness or loneliness. Problems and difficulties arise even during the holiday season. And, for some, the Christmas season evokes painful memories from recent events or the loss of loved ones in the past. Give room for yourself and your family to experience these feelings. Make an effort to work through present challenges and conflicts.

Try to acknowledge the past but look toward the future. Life brings changes. Each season of life is different. Determine to enjoy this Christmas for what it is. Acknowledge the past, whether it was good or bad. But, if you find that this year has been a rough one and you don't anticipate having the best Christmas ever, try not to set yourself up by comparing today with the good times. Try hard to develop and encourage a life of gratitude. No matter what your circumstances, I believe there is reason to be thankful in them. Your circumstances may never change, but your attitude toward them can change … and this can make all the difference.

Try, if possible, to do something for someone else. One of the ways we can demonstrate that we are grateful is to help others. Even if this has been a difficult year for you and your family, helping others will actually help you too as your focus will move from your own circumstances onto serving others. So, enrich this Christmas season for your family by getting involved in serving and helping others. Enjoy activities that are cheap or free. There are many good Christmas-related activities that will add to your family's enjoyment that are either free or low cost, such as driving around to look at Christmas lights and decorations, baking Christmas cakes or going window shopping.

Enjoy a family Christmas tradition. Traditions provide opportunities to keep your family's legacy going. They create meaningful memories. So, from the silly to the sentimental, if your family has some Christmas traditions be sure to include them in your Christmas activity plans.

Try something new. Traditions are great, but sometimes families find themselves celebrating Christmas in exactly the same fashion, year after year. And this can result in your family experiencing a holiday huff. So, think about finding a new way to celebrate the holiday season this year. You may just create a new tradition that will keep going for generations!

Spend money responsibly. The holiday season brings with it a big temptation to spend lots of money especially when it comes to purchasing Christmas presents for your family. Don't be afraid to say no to this temptation, especially if you've been hard hit by the recession. Try to carve out some time for yourself! Don't take on all of the responsibilities of your family's Christmas celebrations by yourself. Share the load. Create some space during the holidays for you to recharge your own batteries.

A poem about the 'Attitude of Gratitude' might help …

If you have food in the refrigerator, clothes on your back, a roof overhead and a place to sleep … you are richer than 75 per cent of this world. If you have money in the bank, in your wallet and spare change in a dish someplace … you are among the top eight per cent of the world's wealthy. If you woke up this morning with good health you are more fortunate than the million who will not survive this week. If you have never experienced the danger of battle unfolding all around you, the loneliness of imprisonment, the agony of torture, or the pangs of starvation ... you are ahead of 600 million people in the world. If you can attend a church meeting without fear of persecution, harassment, arrest, torture, or death ... you are more blessed than three billion people in the world. If your parents are still alive and still married ... you are very rare. If you can read this message you are more blessed than over two billion people in the world that cannot read at all.

Thought for the week

As your thought for the week, look around you and truly cherish and be thankful for all that you have and for all the friends and family that are part of your life. Try hard to nurture a life of gratitude with everyone you meet.

34.

So Others May Live

*R*ecently, while sitting in my office close to the hospital, my thoughts wandered to the well-known lifesavers we encounter every day: firefighters, gardaí, nurses, doctors and those who work mainly in the shadows, who will risk anything and everything to save total strangers under the most extreme and rare of circumstances.

In this category are the coastguard's extraordinary but little-known rescue swimmers. Their helicopter flies over my office regularly as they land at the hospital after saving someone's life. These brave men and women are an elite few, possessing the uncommon physical and mental fortitude to freefall from helicopters directly into raging seas and massive stormfloods to rescue those in harm's way, no matter what the costs.

The coastguard's teeth-gritting training programme is considered the toughest in all of the military. And for those remarkable few who actually make it, what lies ahead are perilous missions in the darkest, coldest, roughest waters known to humankind, where they must battle disorientation, exhaustion, hypothermia and lack of oxygen while trying to help the stranded, the panicked and those who have given up hope.

After seeing the movie 'The Guardian' with my wife not so long ago, we found ourselves inspired by its heroes. There is something inherently precious about the act of saving the life of a complete stranger in a world where hostilities against people we do not know or understand is rampant.

These brave men and women save many lives each year and yet little is known about them and their training. This action drama directed by Andrew Davis from a screenplay by Ron L. Brinkerhoff focuses on the coastguard's elite Rescue Swimmer Programme. Their motto is 'So others may live'.

Ben Randall (Kevin Costner) is a legendary rescue swimmer who has saved many lives and proved to be a miracle worker in the water. However, his courage and willpower are tested when he loses his co-workers and helicopter crew in a crash in the Bering Sea near Kodiak, Alaska. Because he is badly hurt, and his wife Helen (Sela Ward) left him a few months before the accident, his commander (Clancy Brown) gives him a new assignment: teaching the coastguard's 'A' school for rescue divers.

Randall isn't happy about assuming this role, but knows that he has more experience than anyone around. Frank Larson (John Heard), the 'A' school chief, can't wait to see what he does, whereas Jack Skinner (Neal McDonough), an assistant instructor, seems threatened by reporting to such a maverick.

The new recruits are given strenuous physical, emotional and psychological workouts, along with tests to determine their speed, strength and endurance in the water.

Swimming champion Jake Fischer (Ashton Kutcher) singles himself out from the rest, saying he will break all of Randall's records. This young man demonstrates natural leadership abilities but also puts himself first in all situations. He gets in trouble by staying out with his new girlfriend Emily (Melissa Sagemiller), a fiery teacher.

'The Guardian' works as an engaging drama about a middle-aged man's attempt to pass his wisdom and insights on to the next generation. And it turns out that Randall and Fischer have more in common than others know.

Costner excels at this kind of role and Kutcher puts in a stellar performance as a young man who comes into his own under the guidance of an inspiring role model. The rescue sequences at sea are dramatic but it is the inner changes in Randall and Fischer than make the movie worth seeing. Here heroism doesn't mean winning; it means putting others first.

Let's live our lives as brave, unashamed ambassadors of Christ, rescue swimmers in the darkest, coldest, roughest waters known to humankind, where we must battle the trials of life while trying to help the stranded, the panicked and those who have given up all hope.

Thought for the week

As your thought for this week, live and give, echoing the swimmer's motto 'So others may live'.

35

The Real Christmas Spirit

The following is the story of a family that a friend told me about who decided a long time ago that, rather than buying presents and gifts for one another at Christmas, they would buy something more meaningful that would fit into the spirit of a Christ-filled Christmas.

The white envelope

It's just a small, white envelope stuck among the branches of our Christmas tree. No name, no identification, no inscription. It has peeked through the branches of our tree for the past ten years or so.

It all began because my wife Siobhan hated Christmas. Not the true meaning of Christmas, but the commercial aspects of it: overspending, the frantic running around at the last minute to get a tie for Uncle Ricey and the dusting powder for Grandma, the gifts given in desperation because you couldn't think of anything else.

Knowing she felt this way, one year I decided to bypass the usual shirts, sweaters, ties and so forth. I reached for something special just for Siobhan.

The inspiration came in an unusual way. Our son Kevin, who was 12 that year, was boxing at the junior cert level at the school he attended. Shortly before Christmas, there was a non-league match against a team sponsored by an inner-city church, mostly refugees and asylum seekers. These youngsters, dressed in runners so ragged that shoestrings seemed to be the only thing holding them together, presented a sharp contrast to our boys in their spiffy blue and gold uniforms and sparkling new boxing shoes.

As the match began, I was alarmed to see that the other team was boxing without proper headgear, a kind of light helmet designed to protect a boxer's head and ears. It was a luxury the ragtag team obviously could not afford. Well, we ended up walloping them. We took every weight class. And, as each of their boys got up from the mat, he swaggered around in his tatters with false bravado, a kind of street pride that couldn't acknowledge defeat.

Siobhan, seated beside me, shook her head sadly. 'I wish just one of them could have won,' she said. 'They have a lot of potential, but losing like this could take the heart right out of them.'

Siobhan loved kids and she knew them, having coached girls' football and basketball at the local school. That's when the idea for her present came. That afternoon, I went to a local sports shop and bought an assortment of boxing headgear and shoes and sent them anonymously to the inner-city church. On Christmas Eve, I placed the envelope on the tree, the note inside telling Siobhan what I had done and that this was her gift from me. Her smile was the brightest thing about Christmas that year and in succeeding years.

For each Christmas that followed I kept the tradition, one year sending a group of physically incapacitated youngsters to a football game, another year a cheque to a pair of elderly brothers whose home had burned to the ground the week before Christmas, and on and on. The envelope became the highlight of our Christmas. It was always the last thing opened on Christmas morning and our children, ignoring their new toys, would stand with wide-eyed anticipation as their mother lifted the envelope from the tree to reveal its contents. As the children grew, the toys gave way to more practical presents, but the envelope never lost its allure.

We lost Siobhan last year. When Christmas rolled around, I was still so wrapped in grief that I barely got the tree up. But Christmas Eve found me placing an envelope on the tree and in the morning it was joined by three more. Each of our children, unbeknownst to the others, had placed an envelope on the tree for their mother. The tradition has grown and someday will expand even further with our grandchildren standing around the tree with wide-eyed anticipation watching as their fathers and mothers take down the envelope. Siobhan's spirit, like the Christmas spirit, will always be with us.

Thought for the week

As your thought for this week, remember Christ, and 'give' in a Christ-like manner. After all, he is the reason for the season and the true 'Christmas spirit'.

36

A Christmas Story

$\mathcal{T}$he following is a story I received from a close friend whose wife was killed by a drunk driver a few years ago. It is also about the spirit of Christmas and the real love children have for their parents and loved ones.

The doll and the white rose

I hurried into the local shop to grab some last minute Christmas gifts. Christmas was beginning to become such a drag, I wished I could just sleep through it.

Out of the corner of my eye in the doll aisle, I saw a little boy holding a doll. He held her so gently and he kept touching her hair. I wondered who the doll was for. 'Are you sure I don't have enough money?' he asked his aunt.

'You know you don't have enough money,' she said, before asking him to wait as she hurried to get some other items. Now curious, I asked the boy who the doll was for. 'It is the doll my sister wanted so badly for Christmas. She just knew that Santa would bring it,' he said.

I told him that maybe Santa was going to bring it. 'No, Santa can't go where my sister is. I have to give the doll to my Mama to take to her,' he said. I asked him where his sister was.

He looked at me with the saddest eyes and said, 'She has gone to be with Jesus. My Daddy says that Mama is going to have to go be with her. I told my Daddy to tell Mama not to go yet. I told him to tell her to wait 'til I got back from the store.'

Then he showed me some pictures he'd had taken at the front of the store. 'I want my Mama to take this with her, so she don't ever forget me. I love my Mama so very much and I wish she did not have to leave me, but Daddy says she will need to be with my sister,' he said.

The little boy lowered his head and grew very quiet. While he was not looking, I reached into my purse and pulled out a handful of bills. I asked the little boy, 'Shall we count that money one more time?'

I slipped my money in with his and we began to count it. Of course, it was plenty for the doll. He softly said, 'Thank you Jesus for giving me enough money. I just asked Jesus to give me enough money to buy this doll so Mama can take it with her to give to my sister. And he heard my prayer. I wanted to ask him for enough to buy my Mama a white rose, but I didn't ask him, but he gave me enough to buy the doll and a rose for my Mama. She loves white roses so very, very much.'

A few minutes later his aunt came back and I wheeled my cart away. I could not keep from thinking about the little boy as I finished my shopping in a totally different spirit than when I had started.

I remembered a story I had seen in the newspaper about a drunk driver hitting a car and killing a little girl. It said the mother was in a serious condition and the family were deciding on whether to remove the life support.

Two days later, I read that the family had disconnected the life support and the young woman had died. I could not forget the little boy and just kept wondering if the two were somehow connected.

Later that day, I bought some white roses and took them to the funeral home. There, in her coffin, was the young mum holding a lovely white rose, the beautiful doll and the picture of the little boy in the store. I left there in tears, my life changed forever.

Thought for the week

As your thought for this week, make sure you get your fill of the true spirit of Christmas and not the spirit that causes sadness, destruction, despair and death.

37

Know What Is Important

Sometimes people come into our lives and we know right away that they were meant to be there, to serve some purpose, whether it is to teach us a lesson or to help us figure out who we are or who we want to become.

Sometimes things happen to us that seem horrible, painful or unfair, but on reflection we find that without overcoming those obstacles we would never have realised our potential, strength, willpower or heart.

The people we meet who affect our lives, the success and downfalls we experience, help to create who we are and who we become. If someone loves you, give love back to them in whatever way you can, not only because they love you, but because they are teaching you to love and how to open your heart and eyes to things.

If someone hurts you, betrays you or breaks your heart, forgive them, for they have helped you learn about trust and the importance of being cautious to whom you open your heart.

Make every day count. Appreciate every moment and take from those moments everything you possibly can, for you may never be able to experience it again.

Talk to people that you have never talked to before, and listen to what they have to say.

The fisherman

A vacationing American businessman was standing on the pier of a quaint coastal fishing village in Connemara when a small boat with just one young fisherman aboard pulled into the dock.

Inside the small boat were several large salmon. The American complimented the Galway man on the quality of his fish.

'How long did it take you to catch them?' the American casually asked.

'Oh, a few hours,' the Galway man replied.

'Why don't you stay out longer and catch more fish?' the American then asked.

'With this I have more than enough to support my family's needs,' the Galway man said.

The businessman then became serious, 'But what do you do with the rest of your time?'

Responding with a smile, the Galway man answered, 'I sleep late, play with my children, watch football games and take naps with my wife. Sometimes in the evenings, I take a stroll into the village to see my friends, play the guitar and sing a few songs.'

The American impatiently interrupted: 'Look, I have an MBA from Harvard, and I can help you to be more profitable. You can start by fishing several hours longer every day. You can then sell the extra fish you catch. With the extra money, you can buy a bigger boat. With the additional income that larger boat will bring, you can then buy a second boat, a third one, and so on, until you have an entire fleet of fishing boats. Then, instead of selling your catch to a middleman, you'll be able to sell your fish directly to the processor, or even open your own cannery. Eventually, you could control the product, processing and distribution. You could leave this tiny coastal village and move to Galway City, where you could even further expand your enterprise.'

Having never thought of such things, the Galway man asked, 'But how long will all this take?'

After a rapid mental calculation, the businessman pronounced, 'Probably about 15 to 20 years, maybe less if you work really hard.'

'And then what?' asked the Galway fisherman.

'Why, that's the best part!' answered the businessman with a laugh. 'When the time is right, you would sell your company stock to the public and become very rich. You would make millions.'

'What could I do with it all?' asked the Galway man.

The businessman boasted, 'Then you could happily retire with all the money you've made. You could move to a quaint coastal fishing village where you could sleep late, play with your children, watch football games, take naps with your wife and stroll to the village in the evenings where you could play the guitar and sing with your friends all you want.'

Thought for the week

As your thought for this week, know what is important and really matters in your life, and you may find that it is already much closer than you think.

38

The Empty Egg

'The Empty Egg' is a story that was told to me during my teenage years by my Nana Scully.

John Scully was born with a twisted body and a slow mind. At 12 years of age, he was still in second class and seemed unable to learn. His teacher, Doris Miller, often became exasperated with him. He would squirm in his seat, drool and make grunting noises. At other times, he spoke clearly and distinctly, as if a spot of light had penetrated the darkness.

One day Doris called his parents in for a consultation. As the Scullys entered the empty classroom, Doris said to them, 'John really belongs in a special school. It isn't fair to him to be with younger children who don't have learning problems.'

Mrs Scully cried softly into a tissue while her husband spoke. 'Miss Miller,' he said, 'there is no school of that kind nearby. It would be a terrible shock for John if we had to take him out of this school. We know he really likes it here.'

Doris sat for a long time after they had left, staring out the window at the snow. Its coldness seemed to seep into her soul. She wanted to sympathise with the Scullys, but it wasn't fair to keep him in her class. She had 20 other youngsters to teach, and John was a distraction. Furthermore, he would never learn to read and write. Why waste any more time trying?

As she pondered the situation, guilt washed over her. Here I am complaining when my problems are nothing compared to that poor family, she thought. From that day on, she tried hard to ignore John's noises and his blank stares.

New life

Spring came and the children talked excitedly about the coming Easter. Doris told them the story of Jesus and then, to emphasise the idea of new life springing forth, she gave each of them a large plastic egg.

'I want you to take this home and bring it back tomorrow with something inside that shows new life. Do you understand?'

The children responded enthusiastically but John said nothing. Had he understood what she had said about Jesus' death and resurrection? Did he understand the assignment?

The next morning, 21 children came to school, laughing and talking as they placed their eggs on Miss Miller's desk. After they completed their maths lesson, it was time to open the eggs.

In the first egg, Doris found a flower. 'Oh yes, a flower is certainly a sign of new life,' she said. 'When plants peek through the ground, we know that spring is here.' A small girl in the first row waved her arm. 'That's my egg, Miss Miller,' she called out.

The next egg contained a plastic butterfly, which looked very real. Doris held it up. 'We all know that a caterpillar changes and grows into a beautiful butterfly. Yes, that's new life, too.' Little Judy smiled proudly and said, 'Miss Miller, that one is mine.'

Doris opened the third egg and gasped. It was empty and she knew immediately that it was John's. He did not understand her instructions, she thought. If only she had remembered to phone his parents to explain it to them.

Because she did not want to embarrass him, she quietly set the egg aside. Suddenly, John spoke up. 'Miss Miller, aren't you going to talk about my egg?'

Flustered, Doris replied, 'But John, your egg is empty.'

He looked into her eyes and said softly, 'Yes, but Jesus' tomb was empty, too.'

When she could speak again, Doris asked him, 'Do you know why the tomb was empty?'

'Oh, yes,' John said, 'Jesus was killed and put in there. Then His Father raised Him up.'

Doris cried and the cold inside her melted completely away. Three months later, John died. Those who paid their respects at the mortuary were surprised to see 20 eggs on top of his casket, all of them empty.

Thought for the week

As your thought for this week, look at the things in your world that show new life and how we can share that new life or new beginning with those around us who might need new life or a new beginning.

39

The Humble Person

*I*rish people have always been known for their humility. Unfortunately, in modern times, especially during the Celtic Tiger years, we lost some of that. In a highly individualised, competitive world, where we must promote ourselves constantly to get ahead, the old fashioned notion of humility is seen as holding us back.

However, humility is not about putting yourself down or lacking pride; it is not excessive modesty or submissiveness. Rather, we achieve humility when we completely conquer the ego and when we do not see ourselves as superior to others. To be humble, we must acknowledge that we are wrong sometimes. We must accept feedback from others with grace and gratefulness, and try to learn from our mistakes rather than ignoring what we don't want to hear.

We must also take full responsibility for our failures and the consequences of these and not turn the blame on others. A large part of humility is forgiveness. When we learn to forgive those who have wronged us and to apologise to those we have wronged, we step off our soapbox and learn that it is not our role to judge others.

We must also endure unfair treatment with patience and grace, knowing that the world is not always fair but we can do our best to be so. A humble person can be happy for others; can rejoice in their successes and achievements without feeling that they are any less because of them. Gratefulness is another key element to humility. We must try to be grateful for every blessing we are given and every reward we work for. We must also try to be thankful to everyone who helps us along the way, no matter how small or great their assistance may be. Having those who support and believe in you is immensely fortunate.

A humble person is never above helping others, but they do so without shouting it from the rooftops, or looking for recognition or reward. However, perhaps the truest measure of a humble person is the way they treat others. A humble person is kindest to those who have nothing to offer them and will listen with as much attention to a child as to a king.

These are not easy things to achieve; they are high goals to try to reach for, and the true humble person fails to get there sometimes.

Knowing your worth

There is a story about a well-known speaker who started off his seminar by holding up a €20 note.

'Who would like this €20 note?' he asked the 200-strong crowd.

Hands started going up. He said, 'I am going to give this to one of you, but first, let me do this.'

He proceeded to crumple the note up. He then asked, 'Who still wants it?' Still the hands were up in the air. 'Well,' he replied, 'what if I do this?' He dropped it on the ground and started to grind it into the floor with his shoe. He picked it up, now crumpled and dirty. 'Now, who still wants it?' Still hands went into the air.

'My friends, you all have learned a very valuable lesson. No matter what I did to the money, you still wanted it because it did not decrease in value. It was still worth €20. Many times in our lives, we are dropped, crumpled and ground down by the decisions we make and the circumstances that come our way. We feel that we are worthless but, no matter what has happened or what will happen, you will never lose your value. Dirty or clean, crumpled or finely creased, you are still priceless to those who love you.'

The worth of our lives comes not in what we do or who we know, but from who we are. You are special, don't ever forget it!

Thought for the week

As your thought for this week, remember to keep a healthy dose of humility in your lives. By doing so, you are constantly keeping yourself in check and opening yourself up to learning and growing as a person.

40

True Respect Can Only Be Earned

*M*oney makes the world go around but, boy, didn't greed put it in a spin! If greed isn't harnessed and kept under control, it can destroy the world and the majority of its inhabitants before it stops spinning.

Greed is the reason capitalism and socialism function the way they do. The capitalist system encourages greed and depends on the constant race to own the most wealth. Generally, it does so at any cost, including the destruction of the environment and the fabric of society.

Because of some people's greed, the socialist system is marred by those who are never satisfied with their share; those who use whatever chance they get to manipulate themselves into better positions.

But maybe the real problem is the lack of values or, more correctly, the perversion and distortion of values. As long as human beings are valued and celebrated more for their economic success or their power or influence, their spiritual and human progress will play second fiddle.

There are, and always have been, people who feel the need to own more worldly goods than their fellow man. There are those for whom a reasonably comfortable life is just not enough. They feel the need to amass riches by whatever means necessary, so they can compare their wealth with the less fortunate as a measure of how much 'better' they are.

The reason to keep collecting wealth seems to be that having it results in respect. However, gaining respect through the accumulation of wealth is very different to gaining respect by your deeds.

The perpetual struggle for wealth is nothing more than an attempt at boosting personal prestige. It is bringing, and will continue to bring, society down because it will never stop as long as there is someone richer and more influential.

There is a story I heard from a spiritual director of mine about two wolves.

Food for thought

One evening an old Cherokee Indian told his grandson about a battle that goes on inside people. He said, 'My son, the battle is between two wolves inside us all. One is evil. It is anger, envy, jealousy, sorrow, regret, greed, arrogance, self-pity, guilt, resentment, inferiority, lies, false pride, superiority and ego. The other is good. It is joy, peace, love, hope, serenity, humility, kindness, benevolence, empathy, generosity, truth, compassion and faith.'

The grandson thought about it for a minute and then asked his grandfather: 'Which wolf wins?'

The old Cherokee simply replied, 'The one you feed.'

Thought for the week
As your thought for this week, feed what is good in your life.

41

The Taxi Driver

The following story is about showing genuine love to another and was told to me by a lecturer in college.

One summer during my college years, I drove a cab. What I didn't realise before I took the job was that it was also a ministry. Because I drove at night, my cab became a confessional. Passengers climbed in, sat behind me in total anonymity, and told me about their lives.

I encountered people whose lives amazed me, ennobled me and made me laugh and weep. But none touched me more than a woman I picked up late one August night. I assumed I was being sent to pick up some partiers or someone who had had a fight with a lover. However, when I arrived the building was dark except for a single light in a ground floor window. Under these circumstances, many drivers would just beep once or twice, wait for a minute, before driving away. But I had seen too many impoverished people who depended on taxis as their only means of transportation.

I walked to the door and knocked. 'Just a minute,' answered a frail, elderly voice. I could hear something being dragged across the floor. After a long pause, the door opened. A small woman in her eighties stood before me. She was wearing a print dress and a pillbox hat with a veil pinned on it. By her side was a small nylon suitcase. The apartment looked as if no-one had lived in it for years.

'Would you carry my bag to the car?' she asked. I took the suitcase to the cab and returned to assist the woman. She took my arm and we walked slowly toward the curb. She kept thanking me for my kindness.

When we got into the cab, she gave me an address and then asked if I could drive her through town. 'It's not the shortest way,' I told her.

'Oh, I don't mind,' she said, 'I'm not in a hurry. I'm on my way to a hospice.'

I looked in the rear view mirror and noticed her eyes were glistening.

'I don't have any family left,' she said. 'The doctor says I don't have very long myself.'

I quietly reached over and switched off the meter. 'What route would you like me to take?' I asked.

For the next two hours, we drove through town. She showed me the building where she had worked as a secretary and we drove to where she and her husband had lived when they were newlyweds. She had me pull up in front of a casino that had once been a ballroom where she had gone dancing as a girl. Sometimes she would ask me to slow down in front of a particular building or corner and she would sit staring into the darkness, saying nothing.

As the first hint of light creased the horizon, she suddenly said, 'I'm tired now, let's go.'

We drove in silence to the address she had given me. It was a low building, like a convalescence home, with a driveway that passed under a porch. Two orderlies came out to the cab as soon as we pulled up.

I opened the trunk and took out the small suitcase. The woman was already seated in a wheelchair. 'How much do I owe you?' she asked, reaching into her purse. 'Nothing,' I responded and, almost without thinking, I bent down and gave her a hug. She held on to me tightly. 'You gave an old woman a little moment of joy,' she said, 'Thank you.' I squeezed her hand and walked away.

I didn't pick up any more passengers that day. I drove aimlessly, lost in thought. For the rest of that day, I could hardly talk. What if that woman had gotten an angry taxi driver or one who was impatient to end his shift? What if I had refused to take the run, or had beeped once and driven away?'

We are conditioned to think that our lives revolve around great moments, but great moments often catch us unaware.

Thought for the week

As your thought for this week, do the little things well and with genuine love and show that genuine love to others.

42.

Each Day Is A Gift

A 92-year-old petite well-poised and proud lady, who is fully dressed each morning by eight o'clock, with her hair sorted and makeup perfectly applied, even though she is legally blind, moved to a nursing home. Her husband of 70 years recently passed away, making the move necessary.

After many hours of waiting patiently in the lobby of the nursing home, she smiled sweetly when told her room was ready. As she manoeuvred her walker to the elevator, I provided a visual description of her tiny room, including the eyelet curtains that had been hung on her window.

'I love it,' she stated with the enthusiasm of an eight-year-old having just been presented with a new puppy.

'Mrs Scully, you haven't seen the room. Just wait,' I said.

'That doesn't have anything to do with it,' she replied. 'Happiness is something you decide on ahead of time. Whether I like my room or not doesn't depend on how the furniture is arranged, it's how I arrange my mind. I've already decided to love it. It's a decision I make every morning when I wake up. I have a choice; I can spend the day in bed recounting the difficulty I have with the parts of my body that no longer work, or get out of bed and be thankful for the ones that do.

'Each day is a gift and, as long as my eyes open, I'll focus on the new day and all the happy memories I've stored away, just for this time in my life.'

She went on to explain, 'Old age is like a bank account; you withdraw from it what you've put in. So, my advice to you would be to deposit a lot of happiness in the bank account of memories and life.

'And, thank you for your part in filling my memory bank,' she added. 'I am still depositing.'

'Remember the five simple rules to being happy. First, free your heart from hatred. Second, free your mind from worries. Third, live simply. Fourth, give more. And fifth, expect less,' she added.

As Esther Walker once wrote in her *Beatitudes For Friends Of The Aged*:

Blessed are they who understand my faltering step and palsied hand. Blessed are they who know that my ears today must strain to catch the things they say. Blessed are they who seem to know that my eyes are dim and my wits are slow. Blessed are they who looked away when coffee spilled at table today. Blessed are they with cheery smiles that stop to chat for a little while. Blessed are they who never say, 'You've told that story twice today.' Blessed are they who know the ways to bring back memories of yesterdays. Blessed are they who make it known that I'm loved, respected and not alone. Blessed are they who know I'm at a loss to find strength to carry the Cross. Blessed are they who ease the days on my journey home in loving ways and who make each of my days a gift.

Thought for the week

As your thought for this week, remember that each day is a gift and that many of our elderly and aged friends and relatives helped to provide us with such a gift.

43

The Three Trees

*O*nce upon a mountain top, three little trees stood and dreamed of what they wanted to become when they grew up.

The first tree looked up at the stars and said: 'I want to be covered with gold and filled with precious stones. I'll be the most beautiful treasure chest in the world!'

The second tree looked out at the stream that trickled by on its way to the ocean. 'I want to be travelling mighty waters and carrying powerful kings.'

The third tree looked down into the valley below where people worked in a busy town. 'I want to grow so tall that when people stop to look at me, they'll raise their eyes to heaven and think of God.'

Years passed. The rain came, the sun shone and the trees grew tall. One day three woodcutters climbed the mountain. The first woodcutter looked at the first tree and said, 'This tree is beautiful. It is perfect for me.' With a swoop of his shining axe, the first tree fell.

The second woodcutter looked at the second tree and said, 'This tree is strong. It is perfect for me.' With a swoop of his shining axe, the second tree fell.

The third tree felt her heart sink when the last woodcutter looked her way. She stood straight and tall and pointed bravely to heaven. But the woodcutter looked up. 'Any kind of tree will do for me,' he muttered and with a swoop of his shining axe, the third tree fell.

The first tree rejoiced when the woodcutter brought her to a carpenter's shop. But the carpenter fashioned the tree into a feed box for animals. The once beautiful tree was not covered with gold, nor with treasure; she was coated with sawdust and filled with hay for hungry farm animals.

The second tree smiled when the woodcutter took her to a shipyard, but no mighty sailing ship was made that day. Instead the once strong tree was hammered and sawed into a simple fishing boat. She was too small and too weak to sail to an ocean or even a river, instead she was taken to a little lake.

The third tree was confused when the woodcutter cut her into strong beams and left her in a lumberyard. 'What happened?' the once tall tree wondered. 'All I ever wanted was to stay on the mountain top and point to God.'

Many weeks passed and the three trees nearly forgot their dreams. But one night golden starlight poured over the first tree as a young woman placed her newborn baby in the feed box.

'I wish I could make a cradle for him,' her husband whispered.

The mother squeezed his hand and smiled as the starlight shone on the smooth and the sturdy wood. 'This manger is beautiful,' she said.

Suddenly the first tree knew he was holding the greatest treasure in the world.

One evening a tired traveller and his friends crowded into the old fishing boat. The traveller fell asleep as the second tree quietly sailed out into the lake. Soon a thundering and thrashing storm arose. The tree shuddered. She knew she did not have the strength to carry so many passengers safely through the wind and the rain.

The tired man awakened. He stood up, stretched out his hand and said, 'Peace.' The storm stopped as quickly as it had begun.

Suddenly, the second tree knew he was carrying the king of heaven and earth.

One Friday morning, the third tree was startled when her beam was yanked from the forgotten woodpile. She flinched as she was carried through an angry jeering crowd and she shuddered when soldiers nailed a man's hands to her.

But the following Sunday morning, when the sun rose and the earth trembled with joy beneath her, the third tree knew that God's love had changed everything. It had made the third tree strong. And every time people thought of the third tree, they would think of God. That was better than being the tallest tree in the world.

Thought for the week

As your thought for this week, the next time you feel down because you didn't get what you want, just sit tight and be happy because God is thinking of something better to give you.

44

Keep Your Fork, The Best Is Yet To Come

The following story was told to me at a station mass in my house a few years ago.

A woman, who had been diagnosed with a terminal illness and given three months to live, contacted her priest so that she might get her things in order. Duly, he came to her house to discuss certain aspects of her final wishes.

She told him which songs she wanted sung at the funeral, what scriptures she would like read, and what outfit she wanted to be buried in. The woman also requested to be buried with her favourite Bible.

Everything was in order and the priest was preparing to leave when the woman suddenly remembered something very important to her.

'There's one more thing,' she said excitedly. 'What's that?' the priest replied. 'This is very important,' she said, 'I want to be buried with a fork in my right hand.'

The priest stood looking at the woman, not knowing quite what to say. 'That surprises you, doesn't it?' the woman asked.

'Well, to be honest, I'm puzzled by the request,' said the priest.

The woman explained, 'In all my years of attending church socials and gala dinners, I always remember that when the dishes of the main course were being cleared, someone would inevitably lean over and say, "Keep your fork." It was my favourite part because I knew that something better was coming, like Goya's velvety chocolate cake or deep-dish apple pie. Something wonderful, and with substance!

'So, I just want people to see me there in that casket with a fork in my hand and I want them to wonder "What's with the fork?" Then I want you to tell them: "Keep your fork, the best is yet to come."'

The priest's eyes welled up with tears of joy as he hugged the woman goodbye. He knew this would be one of the last times he would see her before her death. But he also knew that the woman had a better grasp of heaven than he did. She knew that something better was coming.

As people were paying their respects by her coffin, they noticed the pretty dress she had asked to be laid out in, they noticed that she was clasping her favourite Bible, and then they noticed the fork in her right hand.

Over and over, the priest heard the question, 'What's with the fork?' And over and over, he smiled.

During his message, the priest told the people of the conversation he had with the woman shortly before she died. He told them about the fork and what it symbolised to her. He told them he would never forget the woman and that he felt they would remember her now too. He was right.

Thought for the week

As your thought for the week, the next time you reach down for your fork, remember that the best is yet to come.

45

Stopped By A Brick

A young aid worker named Padraic was travelling down a street in Luanda, the capital of Angola. He was going a bit too fast in his sleek, white UN jeep which was only a few months old. He was watching for street kids darting out from between parked cars and slowed down when he thought he saw something.

Just then, a brick sailed out and, wallop, it smashed into the jeep's shiny white side door. Immediately, he screeched to a stop, slamming on the brakes and gearing into reverse. His tires spun madly as he brought the jeep back to the spot where the brick had been thrown.

Padraic jumped out of the jeep, grabbed the street kid and pushed him up against a parked car. He shouted at the street kid, 'What was that all about and who are you? Just what the heck are you doing?'

Building up a head of steam, he went on. 'That brick you threw is going to cost you a lot of money. Why did you throw it?'

'Please, mister, please … I'm sorry! I didn't know what else to do!' pleaded the street kid. 'I threw the brick because no one else would stop!'

Tears were dripping down the boy's chin as he pointed around the parked car. 'It's my brother, mister,' he said. 'He rolled off the curb and fell out of his wheelchair and I can't lift him up.'

Sobbing, the boy asked the young development worker, 'Would you please help me get him back into his wheelchair? He's hurt and he's too heavy for me.'

Moved beyond words, the young aid worker tried desperately to swallow the rapidly swelling lump in his throat.

Straining, he lifted the young child back into the wheelchair. He took out his handkerchief and wiped the scrapes and cuts, checking to see that the boy was OK. He then watched the young street kid push him down the sidewalk toward their home in the shanty area of Luanda.

It was a long walk back to the sleek, white, shining jeep.

Padraic never did fix the side door of his jeep. He kept the dent to remind him not to go through life so fast that someone has to throw a brick at him to get his attention.

At times in our lives, we tend to become so wrapped up in other things, we become focused on ourselves or our job and we do not realise there are others around us that need our help. We can react in a negative way to a situation without fully realising or taking the time to look at the other person's situation.

Thought for the week

As your thought for this week, try to be sensitive to those around you and try to become focused on other's needs, so that the bricks in life don't hit you.

46

Things Aren't Always What They Seem

A story is told of two travelling angels who stopped to spend the night in the home of a wealthy family. The family was rude and refused to let the angels stay in the mansion's guestroom. Instead, the angels were given a space in the cold basement.

As they made their bed on the hard floor, the older angel saw a hole in the wall and repaired it. When the younger angel asked why, the older angel replied, 'Things aren't always what they seem.'

The next night, the pair came to rest at the house of a very poor but very hospitable farmer and his wife. After sharing what little food they had, the couple let the angels sleep in their bed where they could have a good night's rest.

When the sun came up the next morning, the angels found the farmer and his wife in tears. Their only cow, whose milk had been their sole income, lay dead in the field. The younger angel was infuriated and asked the older angel how he could let this happen.

'The first man had everything and yet you helped him,' the younger angel accused. 'The second family had little, but were willing to share everything, and you let their cow die.'

'Things aren't always what they seem,' the older angel replied. 'When we stayed in the basement of the mansion, I noticed there was gold stored in that hole in the wall. Since the owner was so obsessed with greed and unwilling to share his good fortune, I sealed the wall so he wouldn't find it. Then last night, as we slept in the farmer's bed, the angel of death came for his wife. I gave him the cow instead. Things aren't always what they seem.'

Remember

Should you find it hard to get to sleep tonight, remember the homeless family that has no bed to lie in. Should you find yourself stuck in traffic, remember the people for whom driving is an unheard-of privilege. Should you have a bad day at work, think of the man or woman who has been out of work for the last number of months. Should you despair over a relationship gone bad, think of the person who has never known what it's like to love and be loved in return. Should you grieve the passing of another weekend, think of the people working twelve hours a day, seven days a week for €1 to feed their family. Should your car break down, leaving you miles away from assistance, think of the paraplegic who would love to be able to make that walk. Should you notice a new grey hair, think of the cancer patient in chemo who wishes he or she had hair to examine? Should you find yourself at a loss, pondering what is life all about, think of those who didn't get the time to ponder. Should you find yourself the victim of other people's bitterness, ignorance, smallness or insecurities, remember that it could be worse; you could be them!

Thought for the week

As your thought for this week, remember that things aren't always what they seem.

47

Treat Others The Way You Would Like To Be Treated

I love inspirational true stories and, God knows, we need a lot of inspiration in our lives and in our world today. The following true story will give you great inspiration for the days and months ahead.

One stormy night many years ago, an elderly man and his wife entered the lobby of a small hotel in Philadelphia. Trying to get out of the rain, the couple approached the front desk hoping to get some shelter for the night.

'Could you possibly give us a room here?' the husband asked.

The clerk, a friendly man with a winning smile, looked at the couple and explained that there were three conventions in town.

'All of our rooms are taken,' the clerk said. 'But I can't send a nice couple like you out into the rain at one o'clock in the morning. Would you be willing to sleep in my room? It's not exactly a suite, but it will be good enough to make you folks comfortable for the night.'

When the couple declined, the young man pressed on. 'Don't worry about me, I'll make out just fine,' he insisted. So the couple agreed.

As he paid his bill the next morning, the elderly man said to the clerk, 'You are the kind of manager who should be the boss of the best hotel in the United States. Maybe some day I'll build one for you.'

The clerk looked at them and smiled and the three of them had a good laugh.

As they drove away, the elderly couple agreed that the helpful clerk was exceptional, as finding people who are both friendly and helpful isn't easy.

Two years passed and the clerk had almost forgotten the incident when he received a letter from the old man. It recalled that stormy night and enclosed a round-trip ticket to New York, asking the young man to pay them a visit.

The old man met him in New York and led him to the corner of Fifth Avenue and 34th Street. He then pointed to a great new building there, a palace of reddish stone, with turrets and watchtowers thrusting up to the sky.

'That,' said the older man, 'is the hotel I have just built for you to manage.'

'You must be joking,' the young man said.

'I can assure you I am not,' said the older man, a sly smile playing around his mouth.

The older man's name was William Waldorf Astor and the magnificent structure was the original Waldorf Astoria Hotel. The young clerk who became its first manager was George C Boldt. This young clerk never foresaw the turn of events that would lead him to become the manager of one of the world's most glamorous hotels.

Entertaining angels

The gospels tells us not to turn our backs on those who are in need, for we might be entertaining angels. Life is more accurately measured by the lives you touch than the things you acquire.

Thought for the week

As your thought for this week, always try to treat others the way you would like to be treated. You might be surprised by the outcome!

48

A Good Boss Cooks Breakfast

One Saturday, I got out of bed early to take my car to my local garage for a routine service. After handing the keys over to the mechanic, I headed to the waiting area, ready to take some time out to catch up on the news.

As I crossed the courtyard the owner, Martin, arrived, carrying what appeared to be some household groceries. During the nine years I have been dealing with this business, I have gotten to know the owner quite well and have always appreciated the great service he and his staff offer in what is a competitive market.

We both stopped for a moment to say hello and I complimented him on getting the chores done before work. He laughed and replied, 'Ronan, this is not for home, it's breakfast for the lads,' before disappearing into the office.

About five minutes later, Martin joined me in the waiting room for a chat and we talked about business in general. I brought him back to the subject of breakfast for the lads. He mentioned that every Saturday he buys eggs, bacon, cheese, tomato and a loaf of bread. He cranks up the cooker at the back of the office and cooks an Irish breakfast icon, the bacon and egg sandwich, for all of his team who are working on Saturday morning.

The reason behind it was simple, he said. A few of the team mentioned that they went to a local café on Saturday morning before work and bought bacon and egg sandwiches and coffee for breakfast. As this was working out to be quite expensive for eight people, he now buys all the ingredients on his way into work, turns on the cooker and puts his cooking skills to the test.

He then excused himself and was off to cook breakfast for all the team.

While cooking breakfast for his team is not such a big deal, I thought this must build staff morale and make his business a happier place to work.

As customers, we have an expectation that we will always receive good service from any business we deal with. However, what determines the quality of the customer service we receive is the attitude of the people who work in the business. As employees, our attitude towards what we do at work is influenced by many things, not least of all how our employer or boss treats us. What Martin was doing is rarely seen in business today. He was being of service to his team and setting an example by cooking breakfast for them.

During my short chat with Martin, I could see he also enjoyed his weekly chef duties and did not view it as anything more than doing something to make the work day all that more enjoyable for his team.

Some may argue that the boss could find more productive ways to add value to his business, but the value of his gesture can easily be seen in the way his team go about their work. In every way, it is a perfect example of genuine and caring leadership, something all bosses should consider as a number one priority in creating a work environment where people are happy, look forward to coming to work and enjoy what they do. The payoff is not just in the job well done, but in the many satisfied customers who remain loyal to the business.

Much to my delight, my car was ready well inside the allotted hour with no major issues to be fixed. As I drove away, I could see a number of the team enjoying their Irish breakfast along with the early morning cup of coffee.

Thought for the week

As your thought for this week, consider playing chef for your employees and see how it affects them, you and the work environment.

49

Dare To Put Action Behind Your Dreams

*W*hy are most of us afraid to follow our dreams? Why do the majority of us find it difficult to achieve what we want, while the minority can somehow set out without so much as a care in the world? What makes some people successful, while others remain simply dreamers?

Is it the difference in their internal makeup? Is it in the way they were raised? The environment they grew up in?

When one studies the lives of 'successful people', one thing becomes evident. These people do not follow a particular pattern. They come from all walks of life and social classes with varying degrees of socioeconomic backgrounds. Some are from affluent families, while others emerge from economically depressed areas and all corners of the earth.

Some of these people are college educated; others learn from the lessons life has taught them. Many learn from a combination of both. However, all of them understand there is no end to learning and that skills have to be constantly upgraded.

While each person has come face to face with giving up, they opted instead to persevere and used it to their advantage. Somehow, they found a way to move past difficulties, trudge ahead and achieve their goal.

And still they plough on, setting new goals and never accepting the status quo. Though they may come from vastly differing backgrounds, each has found within themselves their ability to turn dreams into reality.

You are just like them. You too can be an achiever. Just like these people, you will face adversity. You may have more than your share of shortcomings. You may have lost your job, your way of life or your faith. You may experience an inordinate amount of failure or suffering.

You can still achieve. You have more greatness in you than you know or imagine. It is just a matter of choosing to persevere to your benefit, as all those 'successful people' before you have done.

Nana Scully

My Nana Scully had this to say about life and love:

There is no difficulty that enough love will not conquer; no disease that enough love will not heal; no door that enough love will not open; no gulf that enough love will not bridge; no wall that enough love will not throw down; no sin that enough love will not redeem.

It makes no difference how deeply seated may be the trouble; how hopeless the outlook; how muddled the tangle; how great the mistake. A sufficient realisation of love will dissolve it all. If only you could love enough, you would be the happiest and most powerful being in the world.

Beethoven's music teacher told him he was hopeless as a composer. Walt Disney was fired by a newspaper because he had 'no good ideas'. Thomas Edison's teacher told him he was too stupid to learn anything. Albert Einstein was four years old before he spoke. He stuttered until he was nine. He was advised to drop out of high school and his teachers told him he would never amount to much. Henry Ford's first two automobile businesses failed. Michael Jordan was cut from his high school basketball team. William H Macy's store failed seven times before it caught on. Babe Ruth struck out 1,330 times, but he also hit 714 home runs. Stephen Spielberg dropped out of high school as a sophomore. He was persuaded to come back and was placed in a learning disabled class. He lasted a month. Ray Kroc failed as a real estate salesperson before he set up McDonalds.

Thought for the week

As your thought for this week, dare to dream, but even more importantly, dare to put action behind your dreams.

50

Some Of The Greatest Lessons Are Taught By Children

Some of the greatest lessons are taught by children. Life can be enjoyable if we become aware of the necessity of variety. A child has the desire to have and appreciate variety in life. A child does not think about the silliness or generosity of spirit of its thoughts, or about variety. A child just goes for it.

Anyone who has observed a child for just five minutes (I and my wife had been seeking that for a long while until recently when we adopted our little daughter Mia from Ethiopia) would attest to the fact that a child is continuously seeking variety and change. For a child, life is that particular moment only. It delves into the endless possibilities of finding variety in its day. No wonder children are the happiest people in the world. As we grow up, we tend to become content with routines and seriousness. We run to our office without giving a thought about the cool breeze that morning.

We gulp down our tea without thinking how wonderful it is to taste and feel the refreshing experience of tea. We rummage through the newspapers and forget to feed our minds with positive thoughts. We say the routine 'hello' to many and just pass, when we could really think how blessed we are to know people who respect and hold us in esteem.

Then one day we realise we have grown older, mentally and physically. We become so preoccupied with our responsibilities, chores, problems, future, career, health and family that we forget to enjoy the daily joys of this life.

Where has the child in us gone?

It is so fortunate for us that God has kept that child's spirit permanently inside us, for us to resort to in case we feel we are being bogged down by life. Life need not be bad. Ask your child, or any child, this question and witness their response: 'How are you doing today?'

Their answer will surprise us. They will invariably talk about present things and most probably something positive, creative and challenging; something that gives them aspirations, hope and happiness. We too need to wake up the child in us.

Take time to enjoy the morning breeze, feel the joy of having a wonderful cup of tea with a friend, enjoy the sight of innocent animals playing, the wonderful sight of an eagle soaring, water droplets on the leaves or types of fruit … the list can go on. What an effect these things would create in our minds! Let us remind ourselves of the words, 'Become like children'.

Where is God?

A couple had two little boys, ages 8 and 10, who were excessively mischievous. The two were always getting into trouble and their parents could be assured that if any mischief occurred in their town their two young sons were in some way involved.

The parents were at their wits' end as to what to do about their sons' behaviour. The mother had heard that a clergyman in town had been successful in disciplining children in the past, so she asked her husband if he thought they should send the boys to speak with the clergyman. The husband said, 'We might as well. We need to do something before I really lose my temper!' The clergyman agreed to speak with the boys, but asked to see them individually. The 8-year-old went to meet with him first.

The clergyman sat the boy down and asked him sternly, 'Where is God?' The boy made no response, so the clergyman repeated the question in an even sterner tone, 'Where is God?' Again the boy made no attempt to answer, so the clergyman raised his voice even more and shook his finger in the boy's face, 'Where is God?'

At that, the boy bolted from the room and ran directly home, slamming himself in his closet. His older brother followed him into the closet and said, 'What happened?'

The younger brother replied, 'We're in big trouble this time. God is missing and they think we did it.'

Thought for the week

As your thought for the week, go back to your childhood and try to enjoy the daily joys of life.

51.

Everyone Can Play

When a child that is physically and mentally handicapped comes into the world, an opportunity to realise true human nature presents itself, and it comes in the way other people treat that child. The following story that was told to me recently will help explain what I mean.

Dara the goal scorer supreme

Dara and his father had walked past a park where some boys Dara knew were playing football. Dara asked, 'Do you think they'll let me play?' Dara's father knew that most of the boys would not want someone like Dara on their team, but the father also understood that if his son were allowed to play, it would give him a much-needed sense of belonging and some confidence to be accepted by others in spite of his handicaps.

Dara's father approached one of the boys on the field and asked if Dara could play, not expecting much. The boy looked around for guidance and said, 'We're losing by six points and the game is in the second half. I guess he can be on our team and we'll try to put him in to the forwards in a while.'

Dara struggled over to the team's dug out and put on a team jersey with a broad smile and his Father had a small tear in his eye and warmth in his heart. The boys saw the father's joy at his son being accepted. With ten minutes to go, Dara's team scored a few points but was still behind by three. In the next few minutes Dara was put in at corner forward.

Even though no balls came his way, he was obviously ecstatic just to be in the game and on the field, grinning from ear to ear as his father waved to him from the stands. With five minutes to go, Dara's team scored again. Now, behind by just two points, the potential winning goal was a possibility and Dara based himself just outside of the large square.

At this juncture, do they pass the ball to Dara and give away their chance to win the game? Surprisingly, Dara was given the ball. Everyone knew that a goal was all but impossible because Dara didn't even know how to hold the ball properly, much less connect with the ball.

Hero of the day

However, as Dara stepped up to collect the ball, the defender, recognising that his team had put their thoughts of winning the game aside for this moment in Dara's life, moved back a few steps to let Dara gather the ball so that he could at least make contact and have a clear shot on the goal. Dara swung his right foot and hit a slow ground ball straight past the keeper into the bottom corner of the net.

Everyone yelled and screamed, 'Dara, Dara, Dara, all the way, Dara' and he was cheered as the hero who scored the goal that won the game for his team.

That day the boys from both teams helped bring a piece of true love and humanity into this world. Dara didn't make it to another summer and died that winter, having never forgotten being the hero, making his father so happy and coming home and seeing his mother tearfully embrace her little hero of the day!

Thought for the week

As your thought for the week, try to look at opportunities to realise true examples of how we can make life better for other human beings in our country and world.

52

For Those Of You Feeling Weary – Take Heed!

*T*he following is a list of life's lesson written by Regina Brett, a 90-year-old retired journalist. To celebrate growing older, she once wrote about the lessons life taught her. It was the most requested column she had ever written. So here is the column she wrote in celebration of her 90th birthday. Take heed. It might also help you with some good new year resolutions.

Life's lessons

Life isn't fair, but it's still good. When in doubt, just take the next small step. Life is too short to waste time hating anyone. Your job won't take care of you when you are sick. Your friends and parents will. Stay in touch. Pay off your credit cards every month. You don't have to win every argument. Agree to disagree. Cry with someone. It's more healing than crying alone. It's OK to get angry with God. He can take it. Save for retirement starting with your first pay check. When it comes to chocolate, resistance is futile.

Make peace with your past so it won't screw up the present. It's OK to let your children see you cry. Don't compare your life to others. You have no idea what their journey is all about. If a relationship has to be a secret, you shouldn't be in it. Everything can change in the blink of an eye. But don't worry; God never blinks. Take a deep breath. It calms the mind. Get rid of anything that isn't useful, beautiful or joyful. Whatever doesn't kill you really does make you stronger. It's never too late to have a happy childhood. But the second one is up to you and no one else.

When it comes to going after what you love in life, don't take no for an answer. Burn the candles, use the nice sheets, and wear the fancy lingerie. Don't save it for a special occasion. Today is special. Overprepare, then go with the flow. Be eccentric now. Don't wait for old age to wear purple. The most important sex organ is the brain. No one is in charge of your happiness but you. Frame every so-called disaster with these words: 'In five years, will this matter?' Always choose life. Forgive everyone everything. What other people think of you is none of your business.

Time heals almost everything. Give time. However good or bad a situation is, it will change. Don't take yourself so seriously. No one else does. Believe in miracles. God loves you because of who God is, not because of anything you did or didn't do. Don't audit life. Show up and make the most of it now. Growing old beats the alternative – dying young. Your children get only one childhood. All that truly matters in the end is that you loved.

Get outside every day. Miracles are waiting everywhere. If we all threw our problems in a pile and saw everyone else's, we'd grab ours back. Envy is a waste of time. You already have all you need. The best is yet to come. No matter how you feel, get up, dress up and show up. Yield. Life isn't tied with a bow, but it's still a gift.

Thought for the week

As your thought for the week, look at your life's lessons and see what you are doing about them.

LAST IN CIRC:
10/11/15